"Part odyssey, part travelogue, all heart. This story is crafted with the stuff of the Holy Spirit, where whimsy runs amok!"

Wm. Paul Young

New York Times Best-Selling Author of *The Shack*

"*We Carry Kevan* is a refreshing story of one man's personal journey that unfolds into a community's adventure. Through joy, pain, and friendship, Kevan Chandler reminds us that we are to take every day as a gift from God and live it to its fullest—especially with those we call friends. Through honest reflection and innovative adventure, *We Carry Kevan* will inspire and motivate every reader to live beyond their perceived limits and encourage those we love to do the same."

Steve Bundy

SVP, Joni and Friends International Disability Center

"Kevan Chandler takes readers along on an extraordinary adventure filled with stories of friendship, faith, and perseverance. The courage and determination that this incredible group of friends displayed throughout this amazing journey provide a beacon of hope to all those with disabilities, and I firmly believe that hope is the most powerful gift you can give another human being. *We Carry Kevan* will inspire readers to reach for the stars, reminding us that all things are possible."

Pamela Landwirth

President and CEO of Give Kids the World Village

(A magical nonprofit resort for kids with critical illnesses)

"*We Carry Kevan* is a book of unlikely adventures undertaken on the backs of friends. In these pages we are given an honest glimpse into new yet familiar hopes and struggles, and we are reminded of our profound need for one another. This is a story of selfless love and friendship; a journey where each step is taken in anticipation of the coming kingdom and the day when all things will be made new."

Dr. D. Jeffrey Bingham
Southwestern Baptist Theological Seminary

"In 2012, I was finishing my master's degree at Queen's University Belfast, writing my dissertation on the way in which the church serves as a community of support for families adopting children with complex disabilities. My research pulled heavily from the writings of John, and of how Jesus's encouragement to his church pushes far beyond a desire to live good and moral lives—it is an invitation to radically welcome one another into each other's lives through mutual self-sacrifice and love. In 2012, Kevan Chandler was in the midst of writing a commentary on John, experiencing firsthand what that level of radical welcoming can look like. It is no wonder that God would orchestrate our paths to cross some years later, as we each pursued a deeper understanding of what this type of welcoming could look like for orphans around the world. *We Carry Kevan* is a whimsical, compelling, challenging, and often breathtaking look at the depth of community and love possible if we have the heart to give ourselves to it."

Emily Chapman Richards
Executive Director, Show Hope

"The question of how we might form true Christian community has been a trendy topic in the Western church for decades. *We Carry Kevan* makes me wonder if we've been approaching the question far too abstractly. Kevan's honest and moving travelogue is an essential reminder that shared vulnerability and Christ-imitating service are the real bricks and mortar from which true Christian community must always be formed."

Douglas Kaine McKelvey

Critically Acclaimed Songwriter and Author of *Every Moment Holy*

"Kevan Chandler's story gives me courage, and it reminds me that friendship truly is one of the great creative forces of the world."

Jonathan Rogers

Author of The Wilderking Trilogy and *The Charlatan's Boy*

WE CARRY
KEVAN

WE CARRY KEVAN

SIX FRIENDS.
THREE COUNTRIES.
NO WHEELCHAIR.

KEVAN CHANDLER

WORTHY®
PUBLISHING
New York • Nashville

Worthy
Hachette Book Group
1290 Avenue of the Americas, New York, NY 10104
worthypublishing.com
twitter.com/worthypub

First Edition: April 2019

Worthy is a division of Hachette Book Group, Inc. The Worthy name and logo are trademarks of Hachette Book Group, Inc.

The publisher is not responsible for websites (or their content) that are not owned by the publisher.

The Author is represented by Ambassador Literary Agency, Nashville, TN

Scripture quotations or author's paraphrases are from the ESV® Bible (The Holy Bible, English Standard Version®), copyright © 2001 by Crossway, a publishing ministry of Good News Publishers. Used by permission. All rights reserved.

Cover design: Bart Dawson and Tobias' Outerwear for Books | tobiasdesign.com
Cover photo: Luke Thompson | visualcanopy.com
Author portrait: Noah Huffman | Fort Wayne Film Lab
Print book interior design: Bart Dawson

Cataloging-in-Publication Data is on file with the Library of Congress.

ISBNs: 978-1-68397-317-1 (hardcover), 978-1-54915-068-5 (downloadable audio), 978-1-54601-469-0 (ebook)

Printed in the United States of America
LAKE
10 9 8 7 6 5 4 3 2 1

Your God is watching to see whether you are adventurous.

—J. M. Barrie

CONTENTS

Foreword

I FIRST MET KEVAN after one of my concerts—in Indiana, I think—
many years ago. It goes without saying that he's unforgettable, but
not in the way you might think. Yes, he's in a wheelchair. One of
the fancy motorized ones, no less. Yes, he's always accompanied by
a friend or a retinue of friends he's somehow wrangled into helping him get around. Yes, he has that fiery shock of red hair. All
that might make him interesting, true, but not necessarily unforgettable. Within the first minute of meeting Kevan it was clear that
I wasn't merely encountering a brilliant mind, but a brilliant *heart*.
He was kind, interested, with a quick smile and an engaging way of
listening that made him easy to talk to. Not only that, but he was
hilarious. At the time he had a big bushy beard and was in a metal
band, of which he was the lead singer. He was fluent in nerd talk,
too, and knew more about sci-fi/fantasy and comics than I did by
a long shot. The wheelchair quickly became a footnote in the book
of Kevan himself.

Over the years I would see Kevan again and again. When he and his entourage would approach the stage after a concert, I knew I was in for a good conversation. Once he asked me to pick him up and hold him in my arms, so, with some confusion, I did. He then instructed me to look at the ceiling with an expression of agony, so I did. While I held the pose, his friend snapped a picture. "For a series I'm doing," Kevan explained, "called 'The Death of Kevan.' I think it'll be funny to document a bunch of friends holding me like that." Welcome, one and all, to the wonderful world of Kevan Chandler. And while you may find the joke a bit morbid (I do, and that's why I love it), this story pretty well illustrates part of what makes this book so wonderful. You see, it isn't just about Kevan. It's about his friends. It's about his unique ability to rope people into some cool and crazy idea, and before they know it they're laughing along, caught up in an adventure they never even thought to refuse—and the wonderful thing is, the whole mad scheme is dreamed up and gently proposed by a guy in a wheelchair with a quiet voice and a boyish smile. As I write this, I'm beginning to understand Kevan's affinity for J. M. Barrie. Kevan, both literally and figuratively, is the boy who never grew up.

I love travel stories. I've read several of Bill Bryson's books, Henry Van Dyke's *Out-of-Doors in the Holy Land*, nineteenth century writer Bayard Taylor's *Northern Travel: Summer and Winter Pictures of Sweden, Lapland, and Norway*, David Grann's *The Lost City of Z*, and Jon Krakauer's *Into Thin Air*. I've watched documentaries about Ernest Shackleton's expedition to the South Pole, Alex Honnold's free solo climb of El Capitan, and even Ewan MacGregor's epic motorcycle ride around the world. None of the aforementioned stories are any more courageous than Kevan's. Imagine being confined to a wheelchair for most of your life. Imagine those wheels being your only means of transportation. Other than sleeping or riding in a car, that nest is more or less your constant home, your one safe place. Now imagine saying goodbye to it for weeks on end and placing all your trust in a group of friends who have agreed to literally carry you around for weeks on end to places that, to you, are as inaccessible as the South Pole or the bowels of the Amazon. Kevan is the intrepid sea captain, and his band of brothers is the mighty vessel that carries him into the unknown. If that's not courage, I don't know what is.

But as I said earlier, this journey isn't just about Kevan. It's about those who heaved him onto their backs and bore him for miles and miles, all in the name of friendship, camaraderie, adventure, faithfulness, and a mad scheme to experience this big, beautiful world God made. This story is like the inverse of the photo I took with Kevan all those years ago: they lifted him up and looked at the sky, not with agony, but with joy: "The Life of Kevan."

Kevan and his friend Ben came to my house in Nashville not long ago with the fabled "Yoda backpack." Kevan wanted to see the Warren, this little property where I live. It's not huge, but we have a few acres of woods where I've cut trails over the years. He asked if I'd take him on a tour, and, once again, before I knew it I had agreed and was hefting him onto my back. I'm not sure how much he weighs, but after about ten minutes of hiking it felt like three hundred pounds. I kept walking under branches that were a bit too low, and he would gently inform me that he was being poked in the eye by a hackberry branch. By the time we circled back to the Chapter House, my little writing cabin, I was out of breath and dripping with sweat. With Ben's help I eased the backpack to the floor and then flopped into a chair, pretending not to be winded. Apart from the leaves stuck in his hair and the minor scratches from low hanging branches, Kevan was happy as Peter Pan. I mention this episode to remind you as you read this book what a feat it was for these men to carry Kevan for miles through Paris, or along the English footpaths, or, astonishingly, up the winding stone stairs of Skellig Michael. I couldn't have done it, I tell you, no matter how persuasive Kevan is. These guys are heroes.

I also tell you this because of what happened next. In the Chapter House, just behind the door, is a wall full of signatures. Whenever someone hangs out with me in there, I ask them to sign it as a sort of guest book documentation. I asked Kevan to add his name. I didn't know the best way to accommodate him, so I turned him around in the Yoda backpack and gave him a pen. He signed the wall about three feet from the floor, well below all the other signatures. I immediately regretted not lifting him up so · he could sign where everyone else did, but I tried to play it cool. I offered the pen to Ben, and without a thought, he bent low and signed his name next to Kevan's. When my friend Jason Gray came over a few weeks later I told him how beautiful and Christlike it was that Ben's instinct was to add his name next to Kevan's, and Jason immediately grabbed the pen and did the same. Now there's a cluster of names below all the others, in a place of honor right next to Kevan's.

"Truly I tell you, unless you change and become like little children, you will never enter the kingdom of heaven. Therefore, whoever takes the lowly position of this child is the greatest in the kingdom of heaven." Jesus said that, you know. Lord, teach us to love like Ben, like Jason. Let us stoop to join our friends, and by doing so, to lift them up. It was such a small thing, but in that way Kevan and his friends have taught me to see what I so easily take for granted. That's what this book is about: a widening of imagination—not just Kevan's, which is wide enough to imagine a trip that surely defies what he thought was possible, but Tom's, Ben's, Phillip's, Luke's, Robbie's, Mr. Hill's, all of whom know something about love and brotherhood that they couldn't have learned any other way.

They carried Kevan, and Kevan carried them. I'm grateful to add my signature to that wall.

—Andrew Peterson
The Warren | January 2019

Prologue

FLIGHT

RUBBER BAND AIRPLANES. Do you remember those? Two thin slices of plywood—one cut to look like a fuselage and the other cut like wings. They slipped together, and a set of finicky wheels clipped to the underbelly. A plastic propeller snapped to its nose, and a rubber band stretched from the propeller to the landing gear. Turning the propeller wound up the band, and when released, the flimsy plane took flight, and a boy's imagination soared.

My dad is an airplane mechanic. I grew up going to air shows and flying around in cub planes, watching *The Rocketeer*, and building model aircraft. I have one particular memory of an evening in the late summer when I was eight or nine years old. The sun was setting behind our neighbor's house. Our yard was an ocean of dry Carolina grass, a patchwork of green and faded gold. We have a privacy fence now, but not then. Yards ran together for what seemed like miles (though it was really only two houses in either direction). I remember there was a sense of freedom in the air as we twisted that propeller around and around, the band tightening underneath. My brother, Andrew, knelt by my side and held the plane for me as I helped prep it. Then he stood to launch it high. It zipped around the yard, and we chased after it with silly abandon.

"I wanna throw it," I said, and I tried, but it failed.

I was too short, sitting in my little wheelchair. My throwing arm wasn't that great either. The plane took a dip and crash-landed. I needed height. I needed strength. Or I needed to be content with just chasing it around the yard. You can't do everything, and that's okay, right?

But my dad stepped in. He's a mechanic, after all. He's a problem solver. He undid my seat belt and lifted me into his arms. The world looked different from up there, and I took in the view—at least for a second. I had work to do. I had an airplane to fly! We wound the blade tight, and holding me with one arm, my dad took my hand and we threw the plane together. It was really all his arm, his hand, with mine just along for the ride. The rubber band unwound itself and set the propeller whirring, and the plane ripping across the yard. It flew mighty, wild, and far.

1

POINT OF
DEPARTURE

IT WAS LATE JUNE 2015, a lovely time of year in Fort Wayne, perfect for walking the streets of downtown and getting a last-minute lunch with friends. I was with a couple of young adventurers: Tyler and Drew. We'd run into each other at Fortezza (a coffee shop I call home) and decided orange chicken was in the cards. Over lunch, we shared our dreams and plans. They both had college graduation on the horizon, and the question of what would come next was foremost in each of their minds.

What's next? It's a contagious question, you know, and I was compelled to answer it.

For as long as I could remember, I'd wanted to visit Europe.

I recall sitting at my desk in eighth grade and daydreaming about it. My people, the Chandlers, came from England less than a hundred years ago, and our Christian heritage can be traced back to a Dublin flat in the late 1800s. I grew up in the shadows of literary giants from all over the United Kingdom and other artists from the surrounding lands. So much of who I am today comes from these familial and cultural roots, and my heart has always been drawn back to them. As Tyler and Drew shared their hopes for the future, something within me wandered, as it so often has, into the Old World. The feeling welled up, and I couldn't hold it in anymore.

"Guys," I said, "I'm thinking of going to Europe."

That's how it started. That's how the thought was finally voiced. There was now, in a sense, no turning back. Whether the dream came to fruition or not, it was no longer safely tucked away inside my imagination. The dream was out in the real world, and I was suddenly accountable to it. This was a threshold, a line drawn in the sands of life, and crossing it meant nothing would ever be the same again.

Bolstered by the encouragement of Tyler and Drew, I sent a notice of intent to three friends: Andrew Peterson, Luke Thompson, and Tom Troyer.

To each of them I wrote the following: "I've always wanted to go to Europe, but it seems impossible with my wheelchair. So what if I had a team to take care of me and carry me where I can't go on my own?"

I wrote to Andrew Peterson for his blessing. He's an accomplished songwriter and novelist. He's traveled the world and knows well the cost (more than financially) of such an endeavor. He also knows me. And I trust him. He was the litmus test. If Andrew thought I could pull it off, if he believed in the idea, it would fly.

The dream was out in the real world,
and I was suddenly accountable to it.
This was a threshold,
a line drawn in the sands of life.

I also knew if we were going to do something this crazy, we needed it to be documented. We needed proof. So I contacted Luke Thompson, filmmaker extraordinaire, a man with a keen eye and a good heart. Luke and I had collaborated on smaller projects before, and an opportunity to work together again was welcome.

Then there was Tom Troyer.

* * *

After college, I was living in North Carolina and had a group of friends who were truly free. We played music together, had simple jobs, and lived fully in community. Each week, typically Monday nights, we gathered for a potluck and jam session. Everyone brought food and instruments to share, and we took turns hosting at our houses.

Not many of the houses were wheelchair accessible, but it made no difference to us. We still met at all of them. Some were accessible with ramps, but others boasted incredible flights of stairs. Not a problem. Without a second thought, my friend Hayden (a bear of a man) would scoop me up and carry me inside, leaving my wheelchair outside or in the van.

As Hayden carried me, Tom Troyer would hurry ahead to move obstructing furniture or hold open a door. I'd be set on a couch or on the floor (I preferred the floor), and from there my friends brought the evening to me. Philip Keller gathered food for me or would be the first to come and visit. Tom and Philip shared an apartment with their wives, and two other guys (Luke Carson and Jackson Holt) shared a house just down the street from them. A handful of others came from surrounding neighborhoods and the UNC Greensboro campus nearby. Folks filled their plates and then joined me on the floor, and music came together in the same space. No one thought of these evenings as exceptional. This was our community, living together and loving one another in subtle choices.

One day around that time, Tom and I were driving together to a recording session in the mountains. We had a few hours in the car, and conversation turned to the topic of crazy things we wanted to do in life. The time I had spent with Hayden, Tom, and this group of friends had awakened in me an ever-growing desire not to be limited by my wheelchair. It had been the case growing up—my parents encouraged me to do plenty of things outside of my chair—but these guys took the concept to a new level. I began to realize the possibilities. So I mentioned to Tom that I'd like to spend a day or a weekend independent of my chair.

"What would you do?" he asked.

I wasn't sure, because I hadn't given it more thought than that.

Fortunately, he had something in mind. "If you're going to be out of your chair, we should do something you couldn't do in your chair." His idea? Go urban spelunking. It's like cave exploration, with ropes and hooks and headlamps . . . the whole deal. But instead of caves, we would trek through a sewer system. I wanted to have an adventure outside of my wheelchair, and Tom wanted to explore the Greensboro underground—and what's more, he wanted to explore it with me. So we had a plan.

---

*"If you're going to be out of your chair,
we should do something you couldn't do in your chair."
His idea? Go urban spelunking.*

Jump ahead to a cool April night in 2014. We met at Luke and Jackson's house. Tom put a steel backpack frame on the coffee table, and I was placed in it. As I lay there on my back, with my legs hanging off the table and my arms crossed over my chest like a dead man, the wrapping commenced. We had two ENO hammocks that formed a cocoon around me, securing me to the frame. I faced backward, opposite my carrier. This process was all done with the faithful aid of Philip, along with Luke and Jackson.

Once the makeshift pack was assembled, we set off into the night. I started on Tom's back, and we found a door to the city's plumbing at the bottom of a short flight of stairs. Unfortunately, it was locked from the inside, so Jackson entered through a nearby manhole and navigated his way to open our door. We broke into the underbelly of Greensboro like burglars. We found ourselves in a warm room, well-lit and full of black pipes. *This is kind of odd,* we thought, *and a little disappointing.* Not exactly a Teenage Mutant Ninja Turtles setup. And we certainly wouldn't find Batman, Killer Croc, or Solomon Grundy in these parts, but we decided to go farther in and farther down. As we proceeded, the pipes crossed our path more frequently and inconveniently, until there was little room left to maneuver. The pristine lighting also abandoned us, plunging my friends and me into darkness.

Tom is a tall man, almost treelike. His thick, black beard and hair, along with a set of pronounced eyebrows, are his canopy, and long limbs swing loosely at his sides like branches blowing in the wind. Fitting into smaller spaces is a challenge for him already, but add me to his back and those close quarters were suddenly even tighter.

"We're gonna have to take you down," Tom said to me finally.

A thick pipe hung across our path like a fallen tree. So far we'd climbed over obstacles or crawled under them, but this space was simply too narrow. The guys would have to dismount me from Tom's back and pass me over.

"Let's do what we need to do," I said.

On the other side of the pipe, we came to another open room. It was a wide, circular room, and I half expected guardians to step out of the shadows, surrounding us with dark eyes and raised swords. This room was fairly bright, a kind of oasis before returning to the shadowlands beyond.

Our limber scouts, Philip and Luke, went on ahead and returned with shaking heads. Pipes wove like vines in those halls, and even they couldn't get through, let alone a man with a burden. With this news, we returned the way we came, back topside to find other routes. This wasn't the only sewer in town, after all.

We found another sewer with a different kind of entrance. Philip stayed close to support Tom, who still carried me, as we eased our way down the muddy bank of a freezing creek. Thin branches whisked our faces and legs as Tom's shoes sank into clay and slid on slick leaves. A splash announced our arrival in the creek, and we stared into the gaping maw of a pitch-black sewer world.

With a deep sigh from each of us, we headed inward. The first section was submerged, except for a ledge along the side, so we carefully edged our way into the cave. Tom stepped slowly yet with confidence, and I hung on his back, suspended over the water below. My feet dangled loose like bells from the steel frame, swinging back and forth with a whimsy the rest of me didn't share. *This is adventure*, I told myself . . . *danger, discomfort, chance*. It is a strange paradox to want entirely to be where you are and at the same time not want it at all. This is what adventure looks like from the inside.

---

*Tom stepped slowly yet with confidence, and I hung
on his back, suspended over the water below.
My feet dangled loose . . . swinging back and forth
with a whimsy the rest of me didn't share.*

Eventually the ledge connected to a tunnel and everyone dropped to all fours. I was suddenly on my back, staring up at a concrete ceiling less than an inch from my face. I cringed with the prospects of what could happen—anything from serious rug burn to an all-out broken nose. I had never broken my nose before and didn't plan to do it that night. Jackson crawled up behind us, reaching out to keep his hand like a veil between my nose and the rock.

This tunnel led to a small opening with a manhole overhead. Three tunnels branched off from there, but we decided to linger a moment. Looking up through the manhole, we realized exactly where we were. A street we'd driven on and walked down a hundred times! The revelation brought laughter among us, which led to shouting as we called up to the street and its unsuspecting passersby.

We made our way back to the creek and set off for one more sewer. We found another creek, this one deeper and colder, and it led us into a massive sewer entrance, much bigger than the last. This tunnel was tall enough that we all stood upright, though the ceiling was still uncomfortably close. We walked together side by side with room to spare. Water rose to the shins of my friends, and the darkness of the sludge made it impossible to know what we were slogging through. Phones and flashlights illuminated our path, along with the headlamp we'd brought for the carrier. Graffiti decorated the concave walls with signatures and warnings to turn back now, which we did not heed. How could we?

The passage curved to the right, and we followed it. Our voices, even as low as we kept them, echoed like an army down the watery hall and back. We walked beneath a highway, and the rush of cars rumbled like a distant thunderstorm. Drainage ran from holes in the walls, which added to the mix a subtle sound of moving water. And of course there was laughter. It's one of my favorite things about these guys—the joy in the journey, which they embrace . . . children at play with the scope and strength of men.

* * *

An hour later we sat together at Jimmy John's (the only thing open in the middle of the night). Sandwiches and sodas marked the celebration of our success. Shoes dried under the table as we reminisced. And I don't remember who said it, but someone mentioned spiders, and I flashed a curious look.

Philip scratched an itch and pushed up his glasses. His sharp elbows jutted out as he prepared for another bite of sandwich, "Yeah," he said. "In that last sewer, there were big wolf spiders all over the ceiling."

"How did I miss this?" I cried, realizing how close I'd been to them.

For a moment I was rattled by this revelation, feeling vulnerable to such creatures and what they could've done to my defenseless body. Suddenly I even felt those devils creeping up my spine. A shiver shook them free, though, and I felt instead a profound sense of virility. I'd walked with my friends in the spiders' lair, and we had emerged unscathed and better men than when we had entered. We were changed by survival, shaped by the going, and the world opened up that night to ask the same thing we did: What's next?

PHILIP'S POINT OF VIEW

In remembering our time in the tunnels under Greensboro, Kevan describes his close encounter with spiders and his fear of those creatures. My personal fear was not the spiders but what could happen to Kevan's body.

This was long before we had our official carrying pack, and that night our pack was improvised out of things everyone had lying around. He was wrapped in a hammock, ropes, and tape and stuck to the frame of a camping backpack. It was precarious, and I hoped that his arm wouldn't get caught and break or that anything worse would happen.

When we went through the manhole, I imagined an EMS crew having to figure out why this poor disabled guy was underground. But nothing of the sort happened, of course. What stuck with me from that night is the feeling of camaraderie that comes with doing something out of the ordinary, and I had a renewed admiration for this guy who let his body be put in a pretty ridiculous situation in order to face down a challenge.

2

LAYING OUT
THE FLEECE

It had been a year since we explored those sewers, and the experience resonated between Tom and me like a legend. It was an adventure we'd never forget. So now I asked him, "What if we did that again, but above ground, and in Europe . . . for a month?"

In all honesty, I wouldn't undertake the trip without Tom or Luke. They were essential company, just as Andrew Peterson was essential approval.

One of my favorite Bible stories has been that of Gideon and his fleece. Gideon felt a tug to do something great, but he didn't trust his own gut. So he set out a sheepskin one night and asked God to wet the fleece if the tugging was from him. The next day the fleece was wet on the dry ground—but Gideon wasn't satisfied. So he laid the fleece out again and asked for the opposite, just to make sure. And the next morning the fleece was dry and the ground around it was sopping with dew. Andrew, Tom, and Luke—these men were my fleeces.

I heard back from all three immediately.

Andrew: "This is incredible."

Luke: "Dude, yes!"

Tom: "Oh my."

And we were off. I found two more carriers in my friends Ben Duvall and Philip Keller, and we dove into details. Philip took on the travel plans, booking flights and researching accommodations. Tom spearheaded backpack research and development (we knew we'd need to make some extensive customizations to the makeshift rig we used in the sewer). Luke handled the financial and fund-raising side of things. And Ben kept me sane.

I oversaw the process as a captain might oversee his ship. Along with the physical details, I handled our media presence—interviews, email responses, and online posts. Ben was a close friend, a brother, and he helped regularly with my personal needs as I now lived down the street from him in Indiana. He was scheduled to shower me two or three mornings each week, and we typically hung out the other days too, just for fun. Our lives had become significantly intertwined over the previous years. I trusted him, and he knew me well, so Ben could keep an eye on whether the stresses of leadership were getting to me. And if they did, he knew how to help.

When Churchill was elected prime minister (the first time), Lord Moran was hired as his personal physician. That was his official title anyway. His real job was to monitor the prime minister's mental and emotional health during the onset of a world war. This was Ben's job for me. He was my Moran, caring for my personal well-being as we moved further and further into the stresses of such an all-consuming project. At least there was no world war.

I remember one day during planning, I awoke to what seemed like an endless stream of emails, and my phone wouldn't stop ringing. It seemed everyone had questions—supporters, friends, family, reporters, everyone. It was all good, encouraging even, but oh so overwhelming.

I awoke to what seemed like an endless stream of emails, and my phone wouldn't stop ringing. It seemed everyone had questions.

I had been downtown that morning, but I felt so bombarded that I headed home to try to escape. As I rolled along the river, I tried to slow my heart rate and take deep breaths, and I prayed aloud. "Lord, I've always wanted a platform and audience, and this is awesome, but it's so much so fast and I don't know what to do, I don't know how to handle it well, and I need help, please."

I pray in run-on sentences.

By the time I got home, I had a text from Ben, asking how I was doing. He was up-to-date on how crazy things were, and when it became clear that I was overwhelmed, he headed right over without another question. Ben arrived at my house that afternoon to find me pacing my bedroom, thoughts muddled and tears brimming. I'd always been an extrovert, but this was a whole new level. It was too much too suddenly, even for me. He came in and sat on my bed, fiddling with his phone while I finished writing a text to someone.

As I finished texting, so did Ben, and he looked at me with a cocked grin. Nothing about Ben Duvall is symmetrical—his feet, shoulders, eyes, nose, his grin. From head to toe, the man is thin and crooked and friendly as a '90s comic strip. "You all right?" he asked.

Ben arrived at my house that afternoon to find me pacing my bedroom, thoughts muddled and tears brimming.

I chuckled and shook my head. "It won't stop going off," I said, tapping the screen of my phone.

Ben nodded, then calmly took my phone and set it on my desk. "You need anything before we go?" he asked.

We ended up at JK O'Donnell's, a pub downtown and a regular spot for us. Sometimes you need that quiet time, just you and your best friend at your favorite pub. We sat in contented silence, phone-less, sharing a plate of scotch eggs. For an hour that night, life was normal again, and we were just two dudes at a pub. It was enough to recalibrate me, to stabilize my heart, to organize my thoughts, and to help me jump back into the captain's chair with a level head.

So yes, Ben kept me sane. But we were on our way, and it was going to be a wild ride.

BEN'S POINT OF VIEW

The more I think about the makeup of our team in the beginning, it was easy for me to think that I wasn't really doing enough to assist in getting ready for our trip. I can remember thinking about the guys and all the work they were doing to make this trip happen, and yet here I was with not much to show for helping to get this thing off the ground.

I kept thinking about ways to chip in and had a passage of Scripture come to mind from Exodus 17 where Moses's arms grew tired from holding them up in battle. Since he was tired but couldn't let his arms down, Aaron and Hur came over to assist him by bringing him a stone to sit on and to hold his arms up as the battle went on.

I remember being reminded of this and realizing that this is what I was supposed to do for the team as we prepared for the trip as well as took the trip. My responsibility wasn't necessarily a tangible one, but it was one that definitely had a tangible reward. I was to uphold and encourage my brothers as best as I knew how.

3

PLANS AND PREPARATIONS

OUR COURSE WAS SET: France to visit the home of Django Reinhardt; England to explore Kensington Gardens; Ireland to brave the island of Skellig Michael; and plenty of wiggle room for adventure to find us if she pleased.

As plans came together, training began. Ben was the only one who'd taken care of me extensively, so the others had some catching up to do. We had slumber parties, for lack of a better term, and spent days together to provide opportunities for them to help me. This was anything from eating to restroom needs, showers, and seat adjustments. Add to all of this the carrying. Tom and Philip carried me up and down stairs, held me in different positions, and once we had the backpack, hiked together.

Though I lived in Indiana, I found myself spending time in North Carolina, where my parents still lived, to work with Tom and Philip more closely. One night in January, for example, we stayed over at a guesthouse on the property of my parents' church. It's typically used for hosting missionaries, but that week it was empty. So we got together, the three of us with Luke, for a night of training. We met for dinner first with our friends, the Lees family, at a Mexican restaurant nearby.

Thomas Lees was my roommate after college and was the one who first introduced me to Skellig Michael. He had told me stories of his previous visit to the monastery island and churned in me the desire to go. So now that we were actually going, we thought it would be good to meet with him and his wife, Elizabeth, to have the picture painted afresh as part of our preparation.

Thomas has a disease similar to my own, though it only affects his hands and feet. He regaled us with his adventure, climbing on hands and wobbly knees, step-by-step, to reach the top of Skellig Michael. One false move of his unreliable limbs could have sent him over the edge of a six-hundred-foot drop, but he made it, and he saw the world from a whole new perspective. Then, after taking in every ounce of the view, he scooted himself carefully back down to the port.

As he described that world to us, I could see the island rise up in his eyes. It was an experience that changed him, and I was about to have the same adventure. A shiver of hope ran through my limbs. While I grew up in a Christian home and had a relationship with Jesus, there was something mystical about this place we were going.

It was a pilgrimage in waiting, and on the horizon I could see an encounter with Jesus unlike anything I'd had before.

After tacos, we said good night to Thomas and Elizabeth and headed to the house. Under usual circumstances, I would prefer to train new caregivers with a seasoned caregiver on hand to help out—a combination of a veteran being a safety net as well as a help in explaining how things work. But Ben was nine hours away, and other potentials were unavailable. So, in keeping with the adventurous spirit of the team, we decided I would just teach Tom and Philip myself, no safety net other than Mom and Dad down the road and a hospital around the corner. We figured that on the scale of responsible moves, it was at the very least higher than landing in Paris and figuring it out on the fly.

As he described that world to us, I could see the island rise up in his eyes. It was an experience that changed him, and I was about to have the same adventure.

My daily needs are one thing, and the guys had all done a bit of that. Once I'm in my wheelchair for the day, I'm fairly independent, save for restroom breaks. In such cases, I need help with disrobing, transferring from chair to toilet and back, and then re-robing. Essentially I need help with any action that requires bearing weight, and the restroom is the most intensive in that regard.

At night, when I'm out of my chair, I need a great deal more help. Getting ready for bed means using the restroom, washing up, changing into sleep attire, and getting comfortable in bed (or couch or futon, etc.). Then, throughout the night, I need to be turned from one side to the other. Sometimes this is once or twice, and other times it's something like eight times, along with a restroom visit in the middle. It just depends on the night. And the morning will usually involve a shower, getting dressed, and brushing my teeth, none of which I can do on my own. Finally, I'm back in my chair and on the move again.

We settled into the house, moving furniture to fit our needs and figuring out where everyone would sleep.

Luke wanted to discuss the vision of our trip and his role in filming. He wanted to "launch a campaign," as he called it, to raise money for the endeavor. After all, we were all artists, musicians, writers, and teachers in the public school system. None of us had the funds to make it happen on our own. And our desire was that this experience not be just ours, but be something we could invite others into as well.

When I was a kid, my mom would joke that one day I'd run a hotel because I love having people around. If I plan to meet a couple friends for dinner, we'll end up with a dozen before I realize how many I've invited. I'm always the last to leave a party, and I lock up the church almost every Sunday. As with everything else, I wanted the world to come with me on this trip. We knew we couldn't literally take everyone with us, but a fund-raiser would give people an opportunity to contribute, and social media would allow them to follow along.

Luke had the online stuff all figured out. But he wanted to make sure we were on the same page with filming. My response was, "It's all yours, man." I'd invited him into this because I liked his style and trusted him to tell our story well. As he laid out his ideas that night, sharing examples and walking through processes, my confidence in him only grew. That was the case with all the guys. I trusted them, and that trust only increased as our adventure unfolded.

When I was a kid, my mom would joke that one day
I'd run a hotel because I love having people around.
If I plan to meet a couple friends for dinner,
we'll end up with a dozen.

Next was getting Tom and Philip set for the heavy lifting—me, that is. We joked that this was a double training, getting them ready for the trip as well as child rearing. I started the way I start with everyone, giving them a rundown of what we were about to do, and then I talked them through it as we went, step-by-step. I'm not particularly used to doing this with more than one "student" at a time, so we did everything either twice or in tag-team style.

First, I had them each simply lift me out of my chair and set me back into it. *One arm behind the head, another under the knees. Are you right-handed or left? Okay, now lift with your knees.* They each gave it a go and even talked through it to give each other tips. Then they carried me around the living room a bit. And once they felt comfortable with that (they're fast learners), we transitioned to the great outdoors.

Since we weren't entirely sure what we'd be walking through in Europe, the guys needed to be prepared for carrying me in circumstances more challenging than just a living room. At the very least, we knew our globe-trotting would involve a lot of stairs, whether in Parisian cathedrals or the great Skellig Michael itself.

Tom carried me out the front door and to the right, past the old oak tree, where we found a gravel staircase leading downhill to the church parking lot. It was late, maybe 10:30 p.m., and the area was lit only by the moon and streetlamps over the parking lot. In the darkness, Tom held me cradled close to his chest and took a slow, semi-blind step down, then another and another.

"You're doing great," I said. This quickly became my catchphrase.

Philip and Luke came with us, one in front and the other behind, spotting us as we went. When we reached the halfway point of the stairs, we decided it was Philip's turn. So, in the dark on a gravel staircase, one amateur caregiver passed me to the other. Just as Tom had done, Philip pulled me close, and then he began our descent.

"Oh," I gasped. "You don't have to hold me that tight."

"Sorry, man," Philip said, laughing. "I just don't wanna drop you."

I reassured him, "You're doing great."

It was never a false statement. When I encouraged the guys, it was genuine. Philip might have squeezed a little tighter than needed, but he wasn't doing anything wrong, and it was for a good reason. My encouragement to them throughout training and our trip came from observing their hearts and admiring the work they did. No one is perfect, and I have to remember that with grace as I'm helped by so many. And I'm also constantly amazed by the genius, strength, and innovation of the men who care for me. So when I told them, "You're doing great," it was because they really were.

Reaching the foot of the staircase, we looked at the church and considered climbing up onto the roof. We decided against it, though, realizing we'd made enough silly decisions for one evening. So we ascended the steps, past the old oak, and made our way back indoors.

Next up was the restroom—because I was in need of it.

"We can do this one of two ways," I told them.

Then I realized Luke was filming. He did too. Luke is the sort of filmmaker who naturally has the camera on almost all the time. But some situations are less appropriate than others. This was one of the latter, which I pointed out to him. His response was a goofy smile.

"Don't worry, man," he said with a chuckle. "I'm not gonna . . . well, you know."

I resumed my instructions. "We can do this one of two ways. We can use the toilet or the urinal, which we'll have on the trip."

We agreed we would use a urinal first and save the toilet for our bedtime routine. So one of the guys took me from my chair and laid me on the couch.

Luke went to the fireplace and filmed. He was capturing Philip's and Tom's reactions as they navigated this whole experience for the first time. We'd explored a sewer system together and hung out at each other's houses, but neither of them had ever done anything like this. I think at this point, Philip had only made a plate of food for me at a few potlucks and Tom had helped me in the restroom once before—but that had resulted in me falling into the toilet and one of us bleeding. This was a whole new cup of tea for both of them.

The urinal we're talking about is not the porcelain kind that hangs on a wall, but a plastic vessel one can use while lying down. I'd used it in the hospital a few months prior, when I was dealing with an epic case of what my sister, Connie, called "Butch Cassidy and the Sundance Kidney Stones." After a week of surgeries and excessive hydration, I was sent home. By then I'd come to appreciate the convenience of this device, so the nurse let me keep it.

Tom had helped me in the restroom
once before—but that had resulted in me
falling into the toilet and one of us bleeding.

Everything went smoothly with the urinal. The guys tag-teamed the job, getting my pants down, applying the urinal, waiting . . . waiting, then retrieving the urinal, washing it out, and getting me decent again. They did just fine, and by the time I was back in my chair, you could see the awkwardness dissipating from their faces. Walls were coming down as caregiving was quickly being normalized for two schoolteachers. They were middle-school teachers, so of course there were jokes sprinkled throughout the experience, but we'll skip those for your sake and ours.

After more conversation and a midnight snack, it was time to prepare for bed. Luke headed home, Tom set me solidly on the toilet (redemption for our last mishap), and Philip washed my face. One of them took me to the sectional couch, and the other changed me into pajamas. Before they blanketed me, we went over the process of turning me at night. Mind you, everyone does it differently, so it was really more about me giving them the broad strokes.

"My knees are the rudder," I explained. "Turn them and the rest of me follows. Also, slide the hips back . . . Yep, that'll work."

Tom gave it a go, then Philip. Back and forth I rotated until they both were accustomed to the maneuver. One last turn to actually get me comfortable, along with some blankets to keep me warm. Then the guys got ready themselves.

As the lights went out, sleep came swiftly, but I couldn't help thinking about how crazy all of this really was. We were training for a three-week trip to Europe. I was teaching my friends to help me with all my personal needs, which wasn't new, but this time I was doing it with France in mind, with England and Ireland on the horizon. This was no joke. Not for me. Not for them.

As the lights went out, sleep came swiftly, but I couldn't help thinking about how crazy all of this really was.
We were training for a three-week trip to Europe.

Six hours and three turns later, the sun was up and it was time for us to rise. I've always found it difficult to teach guys the morning routine first thing in the morning. Stiff and groggy, it takes me a bit to really wake up and form coherent thoughts. Add to that a new shower I didn't know how to use and a drain that had a mind of its own. Philip sat me on the toilet while Tom toyed with the shower knobs. There was no hose, so we'd need a cup to pour water over me. One of them found a large plastic cup in the kitchen cupboard. The other set me in the tub once the temperature was suitable, and we were on our way. Scrubbing ensued, rinsing, then out of the tub and into a towel on the couch for drying and dressing.

I did my best explaining the basics of what needed to be done, but a great deal of the morning ended up being these guys just figuring it out. And this proved a perfect opportunity to train them for our trip. Everywhere we stayed would be completely different, and we'd only know so much before arriving. So we had to have the basics down solid but be ready to improvise every few days and work out a new system whenever necessary.

When we eventually got to Europe, the whole team was great at this process—not just figuring out how the shower worked, for example, but also deciding when it was best to shower me and how many guys were needed to do it in this place or that. The knack for innovation was a strength, especially for Ben, but that weekend alone with Tom and Philip helped hone their skills and wherewithal in this regard.

Cleaned and dressed, ready for the day, we straightened up the house and headed out for breakfast. Conveniently, there was a short-order diner just up the road called Breakfastime, where they serve pancakes, eggs, and hash browns—and mac and cheese is listed as a vegetable. We placed our order and reflected on the evening's events in the light of our coming trip. This landed us back at the conversation we'd had with Luke about a fund-raising campaign. If we were going to ask people for money, we needed to come up with a firm number. Philip had a notepad and pen, and we started spitballing. Travel costs, based on our personal experiences; accommodations, not considering at the time that folks would invite us to stay with them for free; food costs, for a group of (at the time) five men in their late twenties.

The night before, Luke had come up with the idea of $30,000 plus $5,000 to cover fees for the crowdfunding site and to allow some wiggle room. After some deliberation at the diner, we actually came up with the same number. Go figure.

After breakfast, the guys dropped me off at my parents' house and went their own ways. It was a sunny afternoon, surprisingly warm for anywhere but Carolina, so I sat quietly on our back deck. I let it sink in, this surreal life I was living, a dream world where globetrotting was common talk and cost was potentially no object. But this was all still just an idea. We'd begun to plan and train, but at the end of the day, it was still just a couple of guys sitting around a living room talking. It was early days, I knew, but would it really come together? And if so, when?

TOM'S POINT OF VIEW

You're probably wondering . . .

Which one of you was bleeding? Did Kevan bite Tom in the arm as he reached for the toilet paper? Did Tom drop Kevan on the tile floor? Did Kevan get half stuck in the toilet seat, necessitating a paramedic be called to the scene . . .

and did they need to use the Jaws of Life to cut the toilet seat? Were Tom and Kevan in some fly-infested Porta-Potty at a music festival, and did Tom's arm get stuck to one of those really too-sticky flypapers and need to be torn off?

Any one of those stories could very well be true. I just wish Kevan wouldn't use the idiomatic expression *cup of tea* while discussing trips to the bathroom. The imagery is unsettling. It isn't sanitary to drink tea in bathrooms, with hand dryers circulating goodness-knows-what all over the place.

4

GATHERING THE CREW

SOME FRIENDS AND I GATHERED to watch the Super Bowl in February 2016, just days before we launched our campaign, which we'd decided to title "We Carry Kevan." It would be an online promotional blitz, centered around the crowdfunding website GoFundMe, where people could give money, leave messages, and find updates on our progress. At this point, our close friends knew about our plans, but the rest of the world did not. Luke and I rode together to the party, and our conversation was tentative, speculative of what the next week would bring.

"I feel," said Luke, "like we're either going to just barely make our goal, or this thing is going to blow up."

The latter was a sentiment among all who heard about our plan, but we didn't want to psych ourselves out. *Let's just get it out there and see what happens*, we thought. I had reservations myself, that tickle of doubt itching my guts and ribs, but I kept going forward. Just as courage is not without fear, so faith is not without doubt, and I did have my fleeces, after all. With every step, the Lord continued to cloak us in favor, enabling us to grow and proceed . . . but I'm getting ahead of myself.

Shortly after the Super Bowl, I went to Nashville for a whirlwind visit. My friend Hayden joined me, and we spent about twenty-four hours there, bouncing around town to catch up with old friends and meet new ones. And all the while, we were back and forth on the phone with Luke, getting things ready for the launch of our campaign that day. I didn't plan it this way, but I think it was good for me to be so busy at such a pivotal moment. Otherwise I would've burned a hole in my parents' carpet, pacing their living room with nervous tension.

It was an early Friday morning, and we were meeting a couple of gentlemen for muffins and then heading to another corner of Music City for burgers with Andrew and his brother, Pete (who insists on calling the backpack a "man-saddle"). I told you it was a whirlwind visit.

Between the two meals, we had thirty minutes open. We found a coffee shop and invested our extra half hour there before lunch. Hayden ordered coffee and took his pipe out on the patio. I set up inside with a cup of tea and my iPad. It was time. Luke had just sent me the link to our GoFundMe page. It was all set to go. I just had to post about it on social media.

I'd voiced an idea to a few friends, and it became a project. Now I had to voice it to the world, to anyone and everyone who would listen. If there was no turning back before, this was a propulsion forward. I stared at the screen. Deep breaths. Deep breaths. I typed out a quick post and added the link. More staring. More deep breaths. Then—before I could flake out—*click*.

I closed the page and sat with my tea for a few minutes, then it was time for lunch.

I'd voiced an idea to a few friends, and it became a project. Now I had to voice it to the world, to anyone and everyone who would listen.

Five minutes later, we were deciding what we wanted on our burgers. Andrew was the first to greet us, and his opening words were, "Hey, did you just launch your campaign?" He'd already seen it! How many other people had already seen it?

"Yeah," I said, laughing. "Right before coming in here."

I determined, for sanity's sake, to avoid checking it the rest of the day. We had lunch, then met a friend for a movie. *Hail, Caesar!* had just come out, and as a general rule, I don't miss the opening of a Coen Brothers film. After the movie, I ran into Andrew again and he had an update.

"Have you checked it?" he asked.

I hadn't.

"You're up to four hundred dollars already!"

We were off and, well, if not running, at least walking.

For the next month, we did local interviews around North Carolina and held Q&A events at friends' houses. Funds came in slowly but surely, and it was looking like we'd get there eventually. I remember having conversations with the team behind closed doors. I felt compelled to stay positive in front of the world, but personally, I was anxious, even discouraged. Everyone believed the project would make a big splash, but so far it had barely made ripples. By mid-March, we'd raised a couple thousand dollars, mere drops in the $35,000 bucket we were trying to fill. I hadn't lost all hope, and I certainly wasn't giving up on this crazy dream, but with each day, it was getting harder to persist.

* * *

I stayed in Carolina for the winter, avoiding the wicked winters of my Indiana home. It proved the most fruitful time of planning for the trip, getting all our ducks in a row, as it were. But as spring eased its way into place, I headed back to Fort Wayne and my ever-faithful coffee shop, Fortezza.

The shop had opened the same weekend I moved to Fort Wayne. I moved to the city to be part of a church, then called Gospel Community, and the owners and staff of Fortezza were friends from the church. It was downtown, just a mile from my house, and the walk to get there was along two of our three rivers. One visit led to two and so on, until it was assumed you could find me there any day of the week. Eventually I was so frequent a patron that I started getting mail there. In fact, about 90 percent of this book was written surrounded by those coffee aromas.

One fun aspect of being a patron of a bustling shop downtown is that you make a lot of friends, and many of them were influential. In this case, my friend Jason came in one day for coffee and noticed me in my usual spot.

"I saw your story online," he said in a jolly tone. "Has anyone from WANE-TV News been in touch?"

This was the local CBS News affiliate, which Jason worked for at the time. I told him we hadn't heard from anyone in Fort Wayne yet, and he jumped into an email. His people would contact me soon, he told me confidently. And they did—about twenty minutes later! Within the hour, the station sent their rookie reporter, Kaitor Kposowa, over to Fortezza to film a quick piece with me. Kaitor was a young buck from Ohio, full of excitement, giddy and nervous on one of his first stories in his new job. We had a great time together as we worked amid the busy sounds of the coffee shop.

The interview lasted maybe fifteen minutes and then he was off to edit. He told me they'd run the story that weekend. The next week CBS national news picked it up as well. Followers and funds for the trip came rolling in, quite literally, overnight.

I was getting ready for church that Sunday morning when my phone rang. I answered the unknown number.

"Is this *the* Kevan of We Carry Kevan?" a lively Australian woman asked.

It was a journalist from CNN, and their story went up that night. On Monday the floodgates opened as Yahoo, MSN, the *Today Show*, the *Huffington Post*, and dozens of their affiliates jumped on the story. Before we knew it, we were halfway to our financial goal. We went from wondering whether the trip would happen to—in the space of a week—buying plane tickets. This was a *huge* boost in morale. One of my favorite parts of our campaign was that people gave twenty dollars here, fifty dollars there, with hardly any big contributions. It wasn't a few people giving a lot; it was a ton of people giving a little! The world was coming around us, supporting us.

One of our favorite interviews was with a man named Hans Heubner. He was a US correspondent for the German news group RTL. This was a unique and wonderful experience from the get-go. While other investigative reporters had scrounged up my email address or phone number, Hans had called Fortezza. I can't help laughing when I remember getting the call from Sean, the owner.

"Hey, man," he said, obviously befuddled. "Some guy just called for you."

"At the shop?" I asked. I was at home, for once.

"Yeah," he said. "He sounded German. I gave him your number."

"Thanks," I replied slowly as my phone lit up with another call.

A few weeks later, Hans flew up from Florida and the team gathered in Fort Wayne for a day of hanging out. I was suited up in the backpack and carried throughout the day by Tom, Ben, and Philip. We walked along the river and explored the "Old Fort," where festivities were going on. Hans was the perfect image of European classiness, with tight jeans, a popped collar, and round glasses that never left his face. The man strutted with a confidence we will never know, for he was a reporter and successful and European. We followed him in awe all day, wishing we could be as cool as he was. He bought us hot dogs and snickerdoodles, which he was infatuated with.

People gave twenty dollars here, fifty dollars there,
with hardly any big contributions.
It wasn't a few people giving a lot;
it was a ton of people giving a little!

"What are these?" he cried with glee. "You guys have to try some!"

"Oh yeah," we agreed. "Snickerdoodles!"

"What?"

"Snickerdoodles," we repeated.

"My mom made them growing up," Philip said.

"Mine too," I added. "You've never had them?"

"No," Hans said. "They're amazing!"

The man was elated.

We ended up in the park, where we met more friends for a picnic. Hans interviewed us all, and his cameraman caught every moment. Then, since it seemed fitting, we walked over to Fortezza and introduced Hans to everyone. While we were there, Sean took me onto his back, went behind the counter, and we threw down latte art together.

As the sun set that afternoon, we sat on my front porch and played music. Hans asked a few more questions and drew out some conversation about faith, hope, and love. Our discussion paused only twice: once to bribe the neighbor kids to be quiet during the interview and again to glare at a passing ice cream truck.

The days to follow were electric. As our audience grew and funds came in, our focus shifted from campaigning to planning the actual trip. Now that the world was watching, it was time to deliver. Philip doubled down on confirming our lodging and transit plans, and Tom and I met more frequently to work on backpack customizations. We also added two more members to our team. Robbie Barnes came on as a fourth carrier, and a Mr. Hill joined as Luke's avuncular production assistant.

* * *

As I mentioned, to fund-raise early on, before the big media boost, we held Q&A events around our hometowns. One of these was a house concert at a friend's home in North Carolina. Josh Stegenga was an old friend from college, and he'd started a house church with his wife after we graduated. They bought a house with a big living room for this purpose, and one Friday night they invited us to come fill it with music and stories about our upcoming trip. Tom played, as well as another Josh, and then I spoke and answered questions. After this our friend David Winbish closed out the night with a Paul Simon cover and several brilliant songs of his own.

Throughout the night, I recognized most of the folks in the

audience—friends from college or my old potluck gang, family members of the musicians, the local neighbors. But there was one guy I couldn't place. I figured he was one of Josh Stegenga's friends and left it there. He was a big guy. He looked like he'd be friends with Josh, who is a tattooed bodybuilder and craft beer brewer. This guy was stocky, barrel-chested, bearded, and southern to the core. He fidgeted with the baseball cap he wore cocked back on his head with sunglasses perched atop the rolled bill.

As our audience grew and funds came in,
our focus shifted from campaigning
to planning the actual trip.
Now that the world was watching,
it was time to deliver.

Halfway through David's set, Josh came and tapped me on the shoulder. I tore myself away from the music and followed him into the kitchen, where this guy was waiting for us.

"This is Robbie," Josh explained to me, gesturing to the bearded man. "He came all the way up from Chapel Hill tonight."

"Wow," I said, shaking his hand.

Chapel Hill was easily a two-hour drive.

"It's great to have you," I said. "What are you in town for?"

"To meet you, man!"

"He came to hear you talk about the trip," clarified Josh. "And I think you might want to hear what he has to say."

There was a twinkle of excitement in Josh's eyes that intrigued me, so I turned to Robbie. He went on to tell me about his own life, how he headed up an outdoor recreation program with his church. He was certified as a wilderness EMT and had led several group hikes around Carolina while also working at an outdoor gear company.

"What I'm tryin' to say," he said in a molasses accent, "is that I'd like to help."

It turned out he was friends with Josh, as well as Luke and a few other guys I knew. He'd come across our story through mutual friends and felt like it was the culmination of all of his passions, to serve others and travel and use his innovative medical skills. Robbie even told us that on a recent hike he'd had to carry a disabled girl through a rough part of the trail.

"So," I said, "this is right up your alley!"

"Yeah, man!" He laughed. "I don't wanna throw off the plans y'all have, but if you're down, I'd love to come and be whatever help I can."

I was thrilled by the prospect and introduced him to the rest of the guys. But we also told him we needed to pray about it. Adding a new cog to the machine wasn't a trivial matter. He understood completely, and there was also the consideration that he was on his way to work in Oregon for the summer, at a job that might or might not allow him time off. We stayed in touch, though. And as the campaign grew, we decided it would be wise to add a fourth carrier. Robbie was our first and only choice, and his new boss in Oregon was completely supportive.

PETE'S POINT OF VIEW

It seems Kevan always blows into town like a whirlwind. In silver Shadowfax (the van) he sails into the driveway from parts unknown, accompanied by an ever-evolving posse of friends who carry and care for him and ferry him to all manner of meetings and clandestine councils. If time allows, we convene for a lunch and a chat and a good deal of laughter before the wind picks up and he's carried away as quickly and as mysteriously as he arrived.

5

GEARING UP

JUST BEFORE I LEFT CAROLINA IN FEBRUARY, I went with Tom and Ben to meet a salesman at REI, the popular outdoor retailer. Tom had told him previously about our trip and he was excited to help us find the right backpack. Sure enough, we found what we wanted in a product from Deuter Sport, a German outdoor company. It would take some tweaking, we realized, but it was a solid frame to start with. Tom then got in touch with Deuter, and they were happy to sponsor us with a major discount and advice on modifications for safety.

Deuter's "Kid Comfort III" model provided a great launch point. The frame was sturdy, the shoulder and belt straps were comfortable for the guys who carried me, and the "bucket" for holding me was something we could work with.

We also connected with a local shop who helped implement our ideas on padding and buckle placement. Modifications were necessary because of two realities. First, the backpack was made for a toddler, and I am much taller and heavier than a toddler. Though I weigh only sixty-five pounds, that's fifteen pounds more than the pack was rated to carry. And being an adult, my anatomy dictates different seating necessities than a toddler's might. Second, my disability limits my mobility and tolerance for bearing weight, so some things folks take for granted, even as toddlers, had to be reconsidered. For example, we had to secure my arms and legs so they wouldn't flop all over like a Muppet's.

With these things in mind, we went to the drawing board, as it were. The backpack came with stirrups, but they hung loose and too high for my use. So those were moved and sewn onto the carrier's belt. This made my feet stable at the carrier's hips and put my knees just behind their shoulders so that the carrier (and I) knew where my legs were at all times. No catching on door frames or railings. I shared my carriers' shoulder width, so if the carrier fit through a space, we knew I could too.

Our next challenge was the seat. The original pack had a sort of strap for a toddler to straddle. This, we learned very quickly, would never work for someone of my size and shape. The rest of the bucket was great, with lateral and chest padding and a high, solid backrest—but the seat was definitely a problem. We took some general principles from my wheelchair, we looked at how guys lift me with their arms, and we considered how I sit best in any situation: knees up, to lean me back more naturally, with weight on the backs of my legs and hips. This would require building a whole new seat.

Finally, the neck. While the seat had a good back that rose high enough to rest my head against, there was no security for my neck. My wheelchair rolls along smoothly, but walking is a bouncy, jostling pastime. And I'm guessing it's a movement the average walker compensates for with his neck muscles to keep his head stable. Because of my disease, my neck muscles aren't that cooperative. So while I can contribute to stability, I can't do it for long before being worn out and done for the day. So we attached a stuffed neck pillow, like the kind you use on an airplane, to cradle my head. It had give, so I could move my head freely, but it provided support so I didn't have to hold my head steady all the time. We also had a traditional neck brace on hand that we could add at especially turbulent times, such as dance parties or long hikes through the woods.

Though I weigh only sixty-five pounds,
that's fifteen pounds more
than the pack was rated to carry.

Then we added a padded wrist cuff to hold my right arm, which has little strength. This cuff attached to a Velcro strip on the backpack, just in front of my chest (behind my carrier's neck), allowing my arm to rest comfortably there. My left arm is somewhat stronger and more mobile, though it tires easily. The backpack came with a loop at the top of the left shoulder strap that I would slip my thumb through to hang on loosely when not using that hand. We're still not sure what this loop was originally intended for, but it came in handy.

We test ran the backpack at REI, but the first time we gave it a real go was in a Greensboro parking garage on a cool March afternoon. We had most of our old group from the sewer venture, and Tom carried me as we climbed a stairwell, level after level, until we reached the open air of the top floor. Tom leaned on the waist-high wall with his elbows, and the wind caught our hair as we peered out over the college town. I laughed a bit to myself. I love "hiking" parking garages, going around and around till I reach the top, but I'm too short in my chair to see over the walls. And now, here I was, in a town I knew so well and even in a spot I could get to on my own, but seeing it from a whole new perspective.

"You okay?" I asked Tom as we returned to make notes at the shop.

My friend hung his head and wiped his brow, eyes closed in defeat. I watched his broad shoulders rise and fall, elbows perched on knees. I had been on those shoulders for the past hour. They rose and fell because of me.

"You okay?"

"Yeah," he said, looking up. "That just took more out of me than I expected."

And this is one of the many things I love about these guys; that it didn't end there.

Tom sat himself upright and sighed. "It's a good thing we have four months to get ready," he said. There wasn't a crumb of doubt in his tone.

From that point on, we made regular walks together as a team, to build strength and a sense of unity. We were a posse of Lost Boys marching to a song through cities and woods, laughing off pain, and bearing one another's weariness, each time going a little farther than the time before. Tom biked to work, Philip joined a gym, Ben took care of me on a daily basis, and Robbie—well, Robbie was all the way out in Oregon paddling boats on rivers, so he was out of reach but perfectly fine and physically ready. As time went on, we grew more confident.

We test ran the backpack at REI,
but the first time we gave it a real go
was in a Greensboro parking garage
on a cool March afternoon.

I, too, had to prepare by exercising and stretching, building my ability to last in the backpack for extended periods of time. It was not, after all, my wheelchair, which is my comfort zone, where I sit best and feel most natural. The backpack, even with our modifications, had its discomforts. As we developed the modifications, someone pointed out to me that there's a difference between functional comfort and couch comfort.

Hiking is never comfortable, it's hard work, but we could design a pack that was comfortable in the practical sense. I wouldn't necessarily fall asleep in it, but I could sit in it on the trails for a few hours and come out on the other end without any pressure sores or major cramps. But I had to stretch, both physically and emotionally, to optimize that functionality so that my legs would rest properly in the pack and my neck would survive the trek. While Tom and the fabricators worked to make the pack more comfortable, I worked toward higher pain tolerance, and we met somewhere in the middle.

We prepared ourselves for the journey ahead, and our financial support continued to flow in. Pete set up a benefit show for us in Nashville, featuring legends Buddy Greene, Ron Block, Wes King, and Eric Peters. Andrew came up to Fort Wayne to headline a benefit show too with Mike Lee, Landon Bailey, and our very own Tom Troyer. And then Tom and I held benefit shows at my brother's house in Ohio, as well as at Prissy Polly's, a local BBQ favorite in North Carolina. With every new day, our spirits were lifted and our dream became more and more a reality.

* * *

In 2012, I went to visit my sister, Connie, in Fort Wayne (long before I moved there). She has always steered me in the right direction, has always been my voice of reason, and that's exactly what I needed then. After years of intensive volunteer work and a full-time internship, I was faced with a difficult truth—because of my disabilities, the career I had pursued would never be attainable. The question came up of what's next.

Connie, my wonderful, sage sister, smirked and narrowed her eyes in wisdom.

"You should focus on writing," she said gently. "You love to write, you love to travel, and you love talking to people. So do that. Write books. Travel. Share your stories and hang out with people."

Little did we know the traveling would be what caught people's attention. She was onto something, though. I was suddenly writing blogs and interviews and articles, and talking to people all day, every day. And they were coming to me! I got to sit back and enjoy the conversations as they happened.

The question came up of what's next.
Connie, my wonderful, sage sister, smirked
and narrowed her eyes in wisdom.
"You should focus on writing," she said gently.

As things came together for the trip and I dealt with this new-found attention, I turned to Andrew once again for guidance. As much as I enjoyed this surge of new popularity, I was having trouble balancing it with normal life. I expressed some concern of turning into a jerk or stewarding the experience poorly. What advice did he have for keeping my head level? I thought he'd give a list of pragmatic steps, like, "Only reply to emails once a week" or "Go for walks twice a day." He didn't. Instead, he told me what I wouldn't have guessed but needed to hear.

"Always be honest with your family and closest friends," he said. "Whatever you do, don't cut them out. In fact, draw them in closer and hang on."

This is the essence of a mentor, and of our unending need for them: that when we ask, they answer with truth we couldn't have known. If we knew it, there would be no need to ask. So ask and accept what comes in the answer, whether or not it's what you expect or want to hear.

"Also," he added, "remember that this experience is a gift from God. He is a good Father, you know, and He's getting a kick out of watching you flourish. And there's grace. So don't get so nervous about screwing up that you miss his gift."

It reminded me of something Eric Liddell says in *Chariots of Fire*. "I believe God made me fast," he tells his sister. "And when I run, I feel his pleasure."

This opportunity was my chance to run. God made me creative and personable, it seems. And when I write, when I travel, when I spend quality time with folks, I feel his pleasure.

* * *

I was in Carolina for a brief visit in May, just a few weeks before our flight date, when we got a call from the shop. The backpack, which we nicknamed "Harv," was done! And not a moment too soon. Tom and his wife, Joy, swung by to get it and came to my parents' house for a test run. Upon their arrival, the terrible truth came out— it *wasn't* done. Not even close. Changes we'd been asking for were disregarded, and other, unwanted changes were tacked on without approval.

Instead of trusting me and making our ideas a reality, the fabricators had decided to do their own thing, which didn't work.

Time was running short, and if we didn't get this huge piece of the trip figured out, everything else could fall apart. What is We Carry Kevan if the "We" has no way to "Carry Kevan"? It was discouraging, to say the least. I knew exactly what needed to be done, but I couldn't do it myself.

Getting me suited up and onto his back, Tom and I took to the woods of my parents' neighborhood, hiking hills, crawling over dead trees, avoiding poison ivy. Joy came with us for support, and to make notes. It was all we knew to do—test the pack in its current state, make notes, and then find ways to make the necessary changes to improve.

Time was running short, and if we didn't get this huge piece of the trip figured out, everything else could fall apart. What is We Carry Kevan if the "We" has no way to "Carry Kevan"?

We walked a mile and a half to visit our friend Charles. Night spread over us as we returned to my parents' house, where Mom had tea ready and Dad had a stack of Styrofoam sheets, differing in size and density, and a knife ready for shaping. This was my experience growing up. I learned how not to give up by watching my parents push forward with trial-and-error solutions. With a *MacGyver* dad and a firecracker mom, there was no giving up in our house, not with three creative kiddos and a couple of wheelchairs in those hallways. In that world, a family can either call defeat or seize the adventure knocking at their door. My parents took the latter approach with unparalleled certainty from day one, and they never looked back.

"Okay, Kevan," Dad said as we walked into the house. "What are you thinking?"

Tom and Joy stayed for a while to brainstorm with us. Then my dad and I went to work on the apparatus. In the thick of it for twenty-four hours, we measured, cut, sewed, and tested until it was right. Finally, on a Saturday afternoon at the end of May, I sat in the pack in my parents' den with a tired smile, secure and comfortable. The backpack was done, and we were ready to go.

CONNIE'S POINT OF VIEW

The best thing about being Kevan's sister is learning the things that make him come alive—private thoughts that make his eyes "crinkle" around the edges, the images that make his grin expand past his ears, the comments that make him throw back his head and laugh. Fascinating people and compelling stories seem to fuel his energy and strength, and I see how that enriches his quality of life, both physically and spiritually.

While so many of us pour into his life by "carrying" him and caring for him, we aren't left empty and dry—he pours right back into us with his natural abundance of love, joy, hope, and light. Kevan has a unique perspective of the world, and it becomes a blessing when he shares it and relates it to others in a really genuine and life-giving way. It is incredible and continues to inspire me, to watch him simply do what delights his heart, to the encouragement of others and to the glory of God—that is worship in its truest and purest form!

6

LEARNING TO FLY

MY PARENTS GREW UP on opposite ends of North America. Dad came from Vancouver, Canada, and was the product of three generations of missionaries. Mom was a new Christian from Fort Lauderdale, Florida, when they met at a Bible school in Chicago and fell in love. After spending a season in Quebec, Mom playing accordion and Dad translating French, the couple moved south to raise a family.

First came my brother, Andrew, a redhead with artistic tendencies. "He's coloring within the lines," everyone noticed in awe while other children were struggling to keep crayon on paper. He also loved to climb trees . . . and to try flying from them too, complete with a superhero cape tied around his neck.

A few years later, my sister, Connie, was born. She beamed with good nature and brought joy to anyone who held her. And hold her they did. The world carried her, cradled her, rocked her, and coddled her. They were glad to do so, and without a second thought. The time came, though, for her to stand on her own. Her first steps were like that of any other wobbly babe. She steadied herself on furniture and pushed her toy shopping cart around the house, happy as can be. This is normal for beginners, but the habit persisted. She never let go.

At around a year and a half old, Connie had a routine checkup with her pediatrician, a kind man named Dr. Schultz. He went through all the protocol. Temperature, hearing, vision. Then he tested her reflexes. A tap on the left knee—nothing. Again. Nothing. A tap on the right. Nothing. He hummed to himself as he felt along her tiny muscles. He calmly left the room for a few minutes and then returned with a note. An appointment had been set for Connie to see a neurologist the next morning.

Tests followed tests and flights from Fort Lauderdale to Boston and back for the next few months, until a diagnosis was made. My parents were brought into a room full of doctors. Their news was sad. Spinal muscular atrophy, a form of muscular dystrophy. The messages for movement were not getting from Connie's brain to her muscles, rendering them weak and weakening still. My parents bowed their heads, and the doctors lowered their own.

"The disease will more than likely be present in any further children you have," said the experts.

"It would be best not to have more," said the doctors in light of the disease.

It's not that the disease is contagious or harmful to others. It has its discomforts for patients and their loved ones, but how much do discomforts determine quality of life? It rendered, at the very least, caution in the minds of the advising doctors. They had valid concerns about the development of SMA and the difficulties it would prove down the road for our family.

"One disabled child will be challenging enough," their eyes suggested. "Don't burden yourselves unnecessarily with another."

But God calls us to be fruitful and multiply. Jesus promises abundant life. The apostle Paul reminds us that outwardly we are all wasting away, but inwardly we can be renewed. Life is a beautiful gift. This was the deep conviction of Peter and Diana Chandler.

It was, in my case, a defining moment. My parents stood at a crossroads. I can see it now: My parents hearing the news. The specialists letting it sink in. Heaven and hell listening with their hosts lining the walls. My deacon father taking the hand of my weeping mother and speaking with gentle certainty to the cloud of witnesses in the room.

---

*The apostle Paul reminds us that outwardly
we are all wasting away, but inwardly we can be renewed.
Life is a beautiful gift. This was the deep conviction
of Peter and Diana Chandler.*

"If you're saying the worst thing that could happen," he said, "is that we have another child like Connie, that would be okay with us."

A year and a half later, on May 19, 1986, I was born. I was diagnosed at the same age Connie was, by the same Dr. Shultz, when I began falling in our backyard. We have one photo of me standing on my own just before I was diagnosed. I stood beside my grandma, grinning ear to ear, and the smiling part never changed. I weakened quickly but laughed all the same and took great pride in making others laugh too. Life had its challenges, but we never let those slow us down or define our family. We lived life to the fullest with costume parties and make-believe games in the yard. Faith and imagination carried us through not to just survive, but to thrive as an adventurous bunch.

When I was four years old, someone donated a wheelchair for me to use. It needed some repairs and adjustments to better fit me, so Dad took it to work and his mechanic buddies pitched in to get it just right. When he brought it home for me to try, I was thrilled but also confused. My dad worked at the airport, repairing planes. He had taken my chair to the hanger to have it fixed up, so . . . where were the wings?

*   *   *

Somehow I survived high school and found my way into college. My courageous sister had moved out on her own, and I followed her lead. She attended the University of North Carolina in Greensboro, about an hour from home, and lived on campus with a few friends.

In my final years of high school, and then in early college years, I spent a lot of time at her dorm and saw glimpses of what it was like to live away from home. I could see from Connie's experience that people could help people, beyond just our parents. And they may not be trained experts, but they could learn if their hearts were right.

My best friend, Zach, also lived on campus at John Wesley College, only twenty-five minutes from my parents' house, and I often spent weekends with him, crashing on his couch. So when I finished my associates of arts at the community college, I transferred to John Wesley and lived on campus as well.

It was difficult for my parents to let us go in this way. Up to that point in our lives, they were the two who took care of us the most. But the short distance and gradual shift helped to ease any concern they had in the transitions. They had also raised us on this trajectory, to live out normal lives as best we could, and this was part of the process. I spent weekends with Zach for a bit and took short road trips with friends in the summer. Then, when I did move out, it wasn't far away at first, and I stayed in touch regularly to calm my worried mom. She and Dad visited often, and I came home for church on the weekends. But then it came time for me to step out a little further.

It was difficult for my parents to let us go in this way.
Up to that point in our lives,
they were the two who took care of us the most.

I was studying for a bachelor's degree in counseling, so the summer of my last year in college I took an internship of prison ministry in Arkansas. Two dear friends, Vineyard and Landon, came with me for caregiving and moral support, one for the first half of the summer and the other for the last half. The final week of my tenure, on my way across the prison yard in the pouring rain, I splashed through a massive puddle and my electric wheelchair decided it had had enough of my shenanigans.

With what little bit of power it still afforded me, I navigated my wheelchair into the barracks of my boys—125 inmates, to be exact. We'd spent two months getting to know each other and friendships had formed, but I'd always been independent. I'd been a counselor to them, a teacher who went home at the end of the day. While personal bonds had developed between us, there were still professional boundaries, and these were convicted felons. As I rolled into the room, however, soaking and slow, all of those boundaries, those expectations and presumptions, fell away. The inmates came running to help, to dry my clothes and warm my bones. Men became brothers that day and throughout the rest of the week.

I put my chair in manual, and the inmates pushed me around the barracks. Counseling sessions, classes, chapel, my office for paperwork. They took turns—sometimes bickering over whose turn it was—pushing me where I needed to go. When the occasion allowed it, I'd sit still while some of them tinkered with the chair's broken motors.

Can you imagine the scene? A scrawny redhead sits in his wheelchair at a card table, pondering over his next move in a game of chess. His opponent sits across from him in a white jumpsuit, tattoos along his neck. On the floor beside them, a man from Detroit lays flat, squinting his eyes, biting his tongue as he works in the tight spaces of the wheelchair's guts. The Detroit man is in his element here, having a sordid history of automotive manipulation. He is in prison for this, in fact, and now redemption comes as he puts his skills to work fixing a redhead's wheelchair.

DAD AND MOM'S POINT OF VIEW

Raising Kevan was always an adventure where we felt he was carrying us along for the ride. We remember the many things he wanted to do growing up and how our family worked together to creatively help make things happen.

One of the first outstanding characteristics we noticed about Kevan from an early age was his magnetic personality, and how he was always surrounded by an amazing number of friends. So it really came as no big surprise to us that he would take off to explore the world like this with a great group of guys. In looking back, it's what we raised him to do.

7

READY FOR TAKEOFF

It was a sunny morning at my parents' house. A white sun rose into a Carolina sky streaked with cotton trails of airplanes long gone. June 18 had arrived, and cars pulled in as our team gathered to depart for the journey. A gravel driveway runs alongside the house so that anyone's arrival is announced by the sound of rock crushed under tires. When I was a child, my dad worked second shift, and I'd stay up to read until I heard that sound, like a reminder that it was time for bed.

That June morning I sat at the dining room table with my mom. We listened to rocks crunching outside. She was remarkably calm, considering the circumstances. Her baby was headed over an ocean, without his wheelchair, and what's more, without her to care for him. I realize this was harder for her than I will ever know and took more courage than I will ever dream of having. We sat together, and she had with her a swath of stationery. She placed it on the table between us.

"I woke up in the middle of the night," she said, "with this quote in mind from Jim Elliot. I haven't read it in years, but the Lord brought it back to memory."

She read aloud to me what she'd written on the paper: "Wherever you are, be all there! Live to the hilt every situation you believe to be the will of God."

Jim Elliot was a missionary to Ecuador in the 1950s, reaching out to a tribe of cannibals who eventually killed him and his team. His wife, Elizabeth, returned to the tribe later, forgiving them and living among them with love. In time, those people came to Christ, even the men responsible for Jim's death. Elizabeth Elliot went on to write her story, along with many other books on being a follower of Christ. She especially enjoyed writing about what it means to be a man of God, referring to Jim's life and his personal notes as a paramount example. Quotes like this from his journal turn boys into men and keep men focused on the straight and narrow.

My mom, like any good mother, had concerns for my safety and worried I'd get arrested in a foreign country. She might have had concern, too, that I'd fall in love with an artsy French girl and never come home. But more than any of that, my mom wanted to be sure that I lived "to the hilt" what the Lord had clearly set before me, that I would know my Creator more fully through this wild ride, and that the watching world would know him too.

My mom, like any good mother, had concerns for my safety and worried I'd get arrested in a foreign country. She might have had concern, too, that I'd fall in love with an artsy French girl and never come home.

I took in the message, letting it fill my heart to the brim. The guys, some with their families, showed up at our house with suitcases in tow and eyes sharp for the adventure ahead. Soon, we had the van packed up, and we huddled in the driveway for a prayer. My dad placed his broad mechanic's hand on my back and committed our team to the Lord. He then kissed me on the head and sent us on our way.

* * *

That night we settled into a hotel by the Atlanta airport and ordered pizza. Actually, we ordered eight large pizzas. We were having company in our little suite.

About a month earlier, we'd heard from a mom, Brandi, in Atlanta whose son had disabilities similar to mine. They'd just gone to Charleston for a family vacation and had to carry eight-year-old Karson through the historic streets. She'd come across our story and wondered about our backpack. Something about their story, or the way she told it, reminded me of my own parents and childhood.

Since we were flying out of Atlanta, I figured it was as good a time as any to meet them.

We had chosen to make the five-hour drive a day early, assuming airport security would have a field day with us. Best to allow plenty of time for that. So here we were with a free evening, the calm before the storm, and a family headed our way: a mom, a dad, and (as it turned out) five little boys. We had a ball with them, eating pizza and swapping stories. They were church planters in the downtown area, so between that and their experience with disabilities, we had plenty to connect on.

Tom and Philip engaged some of the boys with games and talk of Minecraft while their dad, Kris, played on the floor with Karson. Memories came back to me of playing with my dad on the floor when he was a young man like Kris and I was Karson's age. The love I saw between father and son made me miss my dad, but I was thrilled for their family. I felt like I knew Kris and Brandi Parker because I knew Peter and Diana Chandler; I knew the life these kids had because I had it; and I knew the wonderful journey they had ahead of them, growing into men with amazing, loving parents.

Ben was flying in from Fort Wayne to meet us, and the Parkers left just before he arrived. Everyone was together—everyone but Robbie, who had a separate flight from Oregon and would meet us in the Paris airport upon arrival. It seemed things were in order and going smoothly. All we had to do was get through security the next morning, and we'd be golden.

* * *

Sunday morning came, and it lasted for what seemed like days. Continental breakfast, packing bags, cleaning up the room. Our flight wasn't until 6:00 p.m., and we had heard that Atlanta airports boasted TSA lines up to three hours long. With our unique setup— namely, me in a backpack—we planned for twice that. That would put us leaving the hotel around noon. Luke passed the time by interviewing each of us for the documentary, kind of a "famous last words" conversation. I called my parents and a few friends, since contact would be spotty on the trip, and some of the others did the same.

Finally, the time came. We parked my wheelchair in the van and parked the van out of the way in the hotel lot. Then we got me into the pack and onto Ben's back. It didn't hit me then, but this was my good-bye to the wheelchair I sit in almost all day—that I had sat in every day of the past twenty-five years. But we'd used the backpack so much recently, I was used to this transition, and we were in a hurry to catch a shuttle to the airport. The switch in that moment didn't seem like a big deal. It was only later that the weight of it settled in.

It didn't hit me then, but this was my good-bye
to the wheelchair I sit in almost all day—
that I had sat in every day of the past twenty-five years.

Every other time we'd left my chair for the backpack, it was only for a few hours, and my wheelchair was never far away. But it would be locked up in my van four thousand miles away for the next three weeks. It was just me and "Harv" now, with no safety net and no turning back.

We were in a rush, and there was some thrill in getting ready to fly out that distracted me from this reality, but the separation was even less dramatic because of my trust in the guys around me. I found security in my wheelchair. It was familiar to me, and I was in control. But when Ben, Tom, and Philip lifted me out of my ever-present chair and into this new-fangled, homemade contraption, their faithfulness became the catalyst for a new sense of security. And it was a deeper security, built on the love and care of others, proven to be greater than my own strength or any wheelchair I could drive. It was a security that gave me the courage and ability to step out of my comfort zone, on so many levels, and try something entirely different.

A shuttle took us to the airport and everyone on it stared at us. We'd been stared at before in our practice walks, but those were in passing as we went along. This was sitting together in close quarters, and the looks were unavoidable. Considering the public transit systems of Europe, we realized this would not be our last experience like this. A kind, older couple across from us decided to address the elephant in the shuttle, which led to explanations, jokes, and laughter. Soon the ice was broken and everyone in the shuttle was having a good time.

We arrived at the airport about noon and got in line for security checks. I wasn't used to this view, or to waiting in line. There's a separate one, you see, for the disabled, and it's much more streamlined. I gazed out over the maze of people before us, strewn like a necklace around the hall in a confusing zigzag formation. We set down our bags and prepared for a long afternoon of inching along this winding path. That's when we were spotted by a TSA agent and directed to follow her.

She looked old and her blue uniform looked new, probably from particular care given to it. Her eyes, behind thin glasses, left no room for questions, so we followed like she was our mother. What a sight! Five grown men bumbling over suitcases, one toting a ginger on his shoulders, all following a regimented old woman through a busy airport. And lo and behold, where did she take us? The disabled line! We all went through. And should we remove me from the backpack for a pat down? No, no. Security performed their duties just as we were. What we thought would take six hours took less than ten minutes—and we were on our way.

What a sight! Five grown men
bumbling over suitcases, one toting a ginger
on his shoulders, all following a regimented
old woman through a busy airport.
And lo and behold, where did she take us?
The disabled line!

There are two airport scenes we're all familiar with from our favorite movies. One is the running scene: the hero races to catch his flight or the girl leaving on it. The second is its antithesis: the hero has a layover and a montage ensues as he sits in his terminal for an unnatural amount of time. The former would come later in our trip, but today we found ourselves living out the latter. We made a campsite of our luggage and settled down in the far corner of our terminal. Taking turns, we'd run errands to fetch food or coffee. At one point we moved to escape a noisy television, but it was all in vain. At the height of a political rodeo, there was no evading the media—not stateside, anyway. We wondered if that would change once we were in another country. We hoped so.

In our final hour of the terminal wait, Tom and I lay on the floor by a window. The others gathered around us, some sitting, some pacing. Waiting like this is not as romantic as the movies make it out to be, but it was also not that bad. You begin to lose a sense of time and space after the first hour, and by the last one you've forgotten there was a sense to lose at all. And just when your body has decided it doesn't really exist and everything is but a passing dream, that's when they announce your plane is boarding. You collect your things in a haze, file onto the plane, find your seat, and resume your existential stupor for the duration of the flight.

MOM'S POINT OF VIEW

This is a treasured memory for me—sitting at the breakfast table with Kevan as the team loaded the van. Praying for our children (and now our grandchildren) has been my number-one job. So as I prayed for the Lord to banish my doubts and fears over Kevan's big Europe trip, I also prayed for the Lord's will to be done in Kevan's life. Through the tears and some sleepless nights in this process, God then gave an amazing peace to my mother's heart and this exhortation for our dear Kevan.

8

PARIS

THE NEXT MORNING, June 20, we landed in gray and rainy Paris. I sat in a normal chair for the flight, and before we could return me to the backpack, a hyper little woman—round and very French—carted me off in a manual wheelchair. She alone would push it, and there was no arguing this, nor would she hear any argument of my need for the wheelchair. The language barrier and mademoiselle's insistent energy, with which we could simply not keep up, put her in charge until she decided otherwise.

As we flew through the airport, the lady rattled on in French, and Philip used his limited understanding to follow as best he could. Philip is fluent in German and English and has pieces of surrounding languages floating around in his head. This strange and confounding interaction drew forth the bits of French he knew, preparing him for the week ahead.

Like a whirlwind, an airport attendant escorted us through the crowds until we reached customs, where a sea of heads bobbed in slow movements. Everyone who comes through this airport, thousands upon thousands, all funnel through this gate for approval.

The thing about a manual wheelchair versus my powered one, or the backpack, is a matter of control and perspective. In my wheelchair, I am captain, though low to the ground, a height to which I'm accustomed. The backpack leaves me subject to my carrier's whims but my, the view is phenomenal! A manual wheelchair has no redeeming value whatsoever, especially since it's inevitably three sizes too big for 95 percent of truly disabled people. The picture is this, then—a Muppet propped haphazardly in a rickety wheelbarrow, his head tipped back to stare at the ceiling or flopped forward to see nothing at all. He is pushed wherever his pilot deems good or necessary, and the two parties are at angles ill-suited to communication. Place this frustration in a tumult of people and luggage in a foreign land, and you can begin to know the sensory overload going on internally as I floated through the customs crowd.

And aren't we supposed to be keeping an eye out for Robbie around here? How do we communicate this to our spunky little guide? She was sweet, it's true. I don't mean to besmirch her kindness or helpfulness. But she was a lot to take in and—

Robbie! Was that Robbie? A guy who looked like him, anyway, came out of a nearby restroom and crossed right in front of me. He didn't see me (why would he be looking down?), but I saw him.

My head was tipped back, so most of what I saw was just ceiling tiles and fluorescent lights. But someone passed in front of me and was tall enough to fall into my line of sight. And it looked an awful lot like Robbie Barnes. I'm not one to have great response time, but something in me fired all cylinders immediately and I called out, "Robbie!"

A manual wheelchair has
no redeeming value whatsoever. . . .
The picture is this, then—a Muppet
propped haphazardly in a rickety wheelbarrow,
his head tipped back to stare at the ceiling
or flopped forward to see nothing at all.

The man halted and looked left, looked right, just long enough for Luke to see him too. It was Robbie, indeed. He saw Luke and then Tom and Philip. He didn't know Ben yet, or Mr. Hill. Then he looked down at me and leapt with surprise and joy. At last, we were all together; for the first time ever, our team was convened.

Once we were through customs, our attendant released us into the world. Her job was done, so we suited up and got me onto Robbie's back for a crash course. He was ready. The next few hours took us through baggage claim, this Metro, and that shuttle, to a train that carried us to another shuttle. We became swiftly acquainted with the underground system and the attention it demands of its passengers. All of this was directed by Philip and his Moleskine notebook, where he'd written every possible detail for reaching our Parisian flat.

Without a single turnaround we arrived at our Metro stop in Place de Clichy, the heart of Montmartre. As we ascended the stairs, we came out onto a sight I will never forget, for it was a feeling as well, and feelings leave marks. I would give you a description from left to right, but the beautiful cacophony had no direction. Shops and cars and people wound around us like a hundred rivers, and we had emerged at their confluence. Before us, holding it all together, stood a statue, tall and black. It consisted of three figures, one bearing the perch of a mighty fowl and the other two guarding her with ready eyes. We took a moment to gaze upon this image and the moving world around us. It was profound, and just the beginning.

Philip, our fearless leader, had gotten us this far, but we weren't there yet. A block down one of these roads, find the key at the bookshop next door, and up a year of stairs. We came into our seventh-story flat, overlooking Paris for as far as the eye could see, and relieved ourselves of baggage. While the guys brought everything in, I rested. I sat on the floor in the living room and took in the artwork around me, on every wall and in every corner. We'd rented the place from a painter and his wife. Above the fireplace hung a mural some six or seven feet tall of Peter Pan bursting into the Darlings' nursery through the window. This was my kind of place.

Opposite the mural, a narrow staircase spiraled upward. Spider-Man, life-sized, crouched at the top. The staircase led to a balcony-type hallway open to the floor plan. While I waited in the living room below, the guys went to check out our bedrooms upstairs.

"Oh man," Luke said, the first into the master bedroom.

The others joined him. A moment of awestruck silence lingered before someone said, "Go get Kevan." Ben ran down the stairs, giggling with excitement.

"Dude," he said, smiling uncontrollably. "You ready for this?"

Before I could answer, we were halfway up the stairs. As we approached the room, I found the rest of the team sitting on the bed, staring out a window. Their tired eyes were suddenly bright with wonder. The window was a floor-to-ceiling set of doors that led to the world outside. They had opened the window wide and rain pattered on its ledge.

"Here you go, man," Philip said as we entered the room.

Without another word, Ben set me on the floor, my back against the bed. Luke's knee jutted out just to my right. He leaned on it to be closer as we took in the view together.

The window framed a scene like none other. The streets of Paris stretched away for ages, dressed with shops and studios, and they snaked upward to a hilltop just a few miles off. There, at the pinnacle of this tremendous city, stood Sacré-Coeur, the Basilica of the Sacred Heart. A church hall of prayer, committed entirely to that sacrament for the past 250 years, and presiding over all of Paris.

My chest rose as I breathed in the cool air, and I held it for as long as I could. Then out and in again. We sat together, the whole team, and marveled. After a while, the team tapered off to unpack, but Luke and I remained. When we were alone, he slid down to sit beside me on the floor, and we stared out the window together. It had been exactly a year since I'd first suggested to him that we make a backpack and travel to Europe. Neither of us knew if it would actually happen. And now, here we sat. A peace washed over us with the rain outside as we realized where we were, at last.

My chest rose as I breathed in the cool air,
and I held it for as long as I could. Then out and in again.
We sat together, the whole team, and marveled.

"Bro," he said easily, "we made it."

LUKE'S POINT OF VIEW

I can't carry Kevan. Due to a skateboarding injury, tendon damage in my right knee makes it difficult to balance while carrying extra weight. With my camera gear in a roller bag and my head covered by a sheet of plastic, I watched my friends hoist a backpacked man onto their shoulders. Together, we stepped out from beneath the cover of the Paris Metro into the persistent rain.

My job was to document the process, but those first moments in Europe will exist only in our memories; the falling water made sure the camera remained dormant. However, in a trip full of unforgettable experiences, these first few hours in Europe hold a particular vibrancy in my mind. After shuffling across cobblestone streets, squeezing into a questionably compact elevator, and spiraling up narrow wooden stairs, it started to sink in. We were sharing moments that, for countless medical and logistical reasons, should not be possible. And they wouldn't have been, without Kevan's dream.

His courage to prove the power of friendship brought us all to that place, making these memories a reality for each of us. My gratitude for the invitation to experience life in this way exceeds my vocabulary. Now, years later, if I could change one thing about what I said in that moment, I'd only add: "Thanks, dude."

9

THE CITY
OF LIGHT

WE WALKED ABOUT EIGHT MILES TOGETHER before the dancing started.

It was our second day in Paris, and we had one mission— to find the Vivre.fm radio station by 4:00 p.m. for an interview. Philip and I took time that morning to figure out directions, and it was fairly straightforward. Two stops on the Metro, a few blocks of light walking, and we'd be there.

Looking back now, we know the address was correct, and I still feel confident that Philip and I had worked out the directions properly. But something fell apart along the way, and soon after exiting the Metro, we had no idea where we were. A couple of guesses later, a turn or two, a few folks trying to help, and we were truly, hopelessly lost. Maybe it's the romantic in me, but I'd like to think that one of those moments, early on, when we stopped to read a map or ask for help, we did so right in front of our destination. If so, that would mean we were there, left, walked all over the rest of Paris, and then came back. It's a delightfully maddening thought.

I wish I'd kept up with all the places we went, but we were on a mission, so all I can tell you is that we saw more of Paris in those two hours than some Parisians see of Paris in their entire lives. At one point, we passed a row of what we assumed were embassies. Each was its own immaculate palace with a unique flag and a uniquely dressed soldier (or two) guarding the gate. These compounds took up several blocks, and I had to fight the urge to see how close we could get without getting shot or arrested. Fortunately (or unfortunately, depending on how you read the last sentence), I was strapped to Philip's back and subject to his will instead of my own.

Along the way, we did meet several interesting people. A man about our age, who lingered outside a café for no apparent reason, gave us directions and cheered us on after hearing our story of travel and adventure. There was a very nice police officer who was patrolling the entrance to a completely empty thoroughfare and spoke not a word of English. We also met a group of German students, probably early college age, who were visiting Paris on holiday. They enjoyed chatting with Philip in their native tongue. They used their smartphones to help us, as did a bike-taxi driver and a security guard directing traffic in a suit and tie.

The suit-and-tie connected us with a local store owner, who

ultimately got us where we needed to go. It may take a village to raise a child, but now we know it takes a city, three languages, and five iPhones to get a cripple to the radio station. Eventually we found ourselves on the right street, and our radio host, Marion, happened to see us wandering around like a litter of lost puppies.

It may take a village to raise a child, but now we know it takes a city, three languages, and five iPhones to get a cripple to the radio station.

Marion was a dear lady. I'd spoken with her over the past few months in preparation for our visit. She'd interviewed me via Skype about the upcoming trip, and we'd made this plan to do a studio interview while in Paris as a follow-up.

* * *

After the interview, we asked Marion and her staff where they would suggest we eat. It was getting close to dinnertime, so one of them, a genial man with dreadlocks, led us back through the Metro to Place de la République. Along the way, he told us something that made us realize our day was just beginning. It was the 21st of June—summer solstice. And while the sun hadn't set yet, it soon would, and the world would come alive with music and revelry. Our guide described it as a city-wide dance party.

"Gentlemen," Tom exclaimed with childlike enthusiasm, "this is the night to be in Paris!"

Suddenly the weariness of wandering those eight miles meant very little. The streets were filling, tents and stages were being set up, and music was beginning.

We found a hole-in-the-wall kabob shop (Turkish fare) and got our fill before setting out to join the festivities. In the short time we were tucked away, eating, the city burst to life, like a sleight of hand when we weren't looking. When we stepped out into the street, we found a massive crowd and a cacophony of tunes.

To our right stood several tents with DJs and MCs. To our left, we saw a half-pipe with skaters and bikers doing tricks in the sky. I opted to visit the half-pipe first, and it was fun to just walk up, stand in the crowd, and watch. No wheelchair. I didn't have to push my way to the front or find a vantage point. I could see from anywhere we stood, and I could see it all, from the base of the ramp to the peak of the skater's ascent.

There was so much going on that our team scattered, some drawn to other attractions, some going off in search of drinks. Luke hung back and shot video of the half-pipe scene. Robbie carried me, and we stood in the crowd watching skaters defy the law of gravity. After a while, we wandered through the crowd until our gang eventually regrouped.

As we lingered together in the square, considering which direction to go, a little boy ran up to us. What his story was, we couldn't quite decide, but if there ever was a Parisian Lost Boy, he fit the bill. Tiny, wide-eyed, mischievous, with a tank top, shorts, and . . . maybe shoes? He was funny in that he joined our group like he was part of the conversation, silently glancing at each of us like old friends and complete strangers at once. A handful of times he disappeared (perhaps reporting back to Peter) and then reappeared as if he'd never left. Lost Boy? More of a sprite or brownie, now that I think of it. He really liked Philip (maybe he could sense Philip's teacherly manner), but he was also taken with me: the strange man in a backpack, smiling down on him.

I don't know if he had to build up the courage or if he finally found the right words to say, but he suddenly pointed up at me and cried with glee, "Petite! Petite!" Then he ran off as before, and we never saw him again.

I don't know if he had to build up the courage
or if he finally found the right words to say,
but he suddenly pointed up at me
and cried with glee, "Petite! Petite!"

At the center of Place de la République is a monument some one hundred feet tall with a woman (Marianne) at its peak. A mighty lion stands guard at the base. Both are pitch black and powerful in their stance. This is a monument to French ideals and has stood for two hundred years, but the once glorious statue was marred. Graffiti, photos, candles covered its surface, along with plastered notebook paper grieving the loss of friends and innocence. After the terrorist attacks on Paris earlier that year, the natives had turned this memorial of French ideals into a mausoleum, reminding us of mortality and the darkness of man. But it also begged for hope in its mourning. "Amour" was scrawled across the lion, with French flags and peace symbols wrapped around his chest.

The locals lounged on the statue, sitting around and atop it like it was their own front porch. They ate and drank, sang songs and played games like there was no tomorrow and no one cared. It was a sobering vision, this monument of turmoil, peopled with life and carefree silliness. I couldn't look away from the dichotomy.

It was Philip's turn to carry me again, and just in time too. As we meandered through the square, he mentioned going to hear a Christian group singing somewhere. He had seen them earlier and wanted to go back. I was up for it, though a bit trepidatious, so off we went.

Now, I don't know about you, but my presumptions are skewed by my culture, so when Philip said "a Christian group singing," I imagined a gaggle of polo-shirted guitar players singing, "Shout to the Lord." I'm ashamed this was my mind-set. I thought, *We'll just stay for a minute and bow out graciously*. But what we came upon was something else entirely.

Drums filled our ears. Rhythms of life and joy bounced off the pavement like soccer balls and surrounded us. And there was dancing! A circle of African people of all ages huddled and spread, huddled and spread. They moved not just their feet but their whole bodies, and with such vitality and as a unit that they seemed "in one accord," as Scripture would put it. And their singing was tribal, an uproar of praise, with call-and-response lines shouted by one through a megaphone and answered by the swarm around her. It was in the midst of this dancing that I realized only one drum was responsible for the untamable beat—one man, sitting on the ground with a bucket overturned between his knees. His arms flew high like the skaters we'd just left and came slapping down on the drum's surface, only to ricochet back into the air overhead.

My soul was revived. The sights and sounds were exciting, but the spirit of it all was what made me new in that moment. It was the Holy Spirit, present and enjoying himself among this bundle of believers. Philip, too, was inspired. I encouraged him to go into the circle and join in the celebration. He and I ran into the crowd together and danced among our unmet friends. No one stopped to stare at a scrawny white boy on the back of another scrawny white boy. No one gave it a second thought. We were part of the party, part of the family.

My soul was revived. The sights and sounds were exciting, but the spirit of it all was what made me new in that moment. It was the Holy Spirit, present and enjoying himself among this bundle of believers.

"Alle-LU-ia!" shouted the leader, and we all responded, again and again. For me, it was dizzying and jolting, but I let myself fall into it until the whirling became a natural, fluid motion in tandem with the music, the people, and the heart of the worship experience. This is, I assume, the key to dancing—to "let go"—and I've experienced it to an extent in my wheelchair, at concerts or wedding receptions. But this was another level. Dancing is communal.

Dancing is intimate. Dancing is an ocean, and I was lost within its waves.

After a few numbers, we slipped out of the circle and moved on to see what might be next. Notes of big band jazz moved like a tide over the next block. It was coming from across the street, and we made our way toward it. As we got closer, however, we found the band was inside a restaurant and unavailable to us, unless we wanted to invest financially and gluttonously. I'm sad to say we moved on.

By this point in the evening, my long day in the backpack had begun to wear on me. My hips and tailbone were aching, and we had to stop often on the sidewalk and make adjustments. Sometimes Robbie would lift me from under the arms, relieving pressure on those seated regions. My size and shape might have conveyed the image of a redheaded scarecrow hung on a busy street corner. As we rested my weary buttocks, Tom offered his shoulders as the next carrier.

"Let's have a talk," I said, motioning for him to join me on the ground.

He squatted down beside me with a goofy grin. The reason we needed to talk was this: Tom is a loose-limbed, swaggering, free-spirited man—with or without alcohol in his system. And tonight he had been drinking, not to excess, but enough for me to wonder. The question had to be asked. I placed my hand on his shoulder.

"You've been drinking," I said.

"And you're wondering if I'm too drunk to carry you responsibly," he filled in, unoffended.

He took a second to think and then nodded. He stood up, stretched, and found a split in the sidewalk. A straight line. He spread his arms wide and slowly walked the concrete tightrope, glancing down solemnly at the hundred-foot drop into inebriated failure.

The question had to be asked. I placed my hand
on his shoulder. "You've been drinking," I said.
"And you're wondering if I'm too drunk
to carry you responsibly," he filled in, unoffended.

He crossed the imaginary chasm like his life depended on it and, with a lanky return to my side, said confidently, "Yep, I'm good to go."

He explained to me later that he knew full-well his condition and capability, but understanding my sentiments, he felt it appropriate to confirm his sobriety for my comfort. It's a funny thing, to trust another person with your life while also working with them to be responsible. The result (when done properly) is a moment like this: a beautiful crossroads of honesty and empathy.

So I was up and onto Tom's back, ready to take on the world. He was itching to dance, and I was right there with him. As the sun settled into a blue dusk, we went a bit farther through the crowded, living, breathing city. What our guide had said earlier was true. Music and dancing engulfed us no matter where we went. As far as the eye could see, as far as the ear could hear, in every direction there was life—and we were part of it.

We slowed in front of a café, where Mr. Hill stepped in to make a quick purchase. As we waited, Tom noticed a tree stump protruding from the sidewalk and decided to step on it. We posed for fun and gave a few gyrations while we were at it. Mostly we enjoyed the view, looking down the street at the various scenes. I imagine we were a spectacle, alighting that stump casually in front of the busy café. One woman came and praised us for our boldness and obvious love of life. It turned out that she was from California, visiting Paris with her boyfriend. We explained our travels as well, and she was thrilled. This was one of countless occasions when we got to share our story in detail to passersby, and I loved seeing how encouraged they were by it. My hope is that these conversations were not quickly forgotten but will find their way into other conversations and experiences for years to come.

There was so much going on around us that, as Tom and I discovered, the best thing to do was to take it in as we passed without stopping. Every once in a while we had to pause to shift me, relieving pressure on my tailbone. But I encouraged Tom to keep moving. "I hurt less when I'm dancing," I told him. When we were bouncing and twisting, jiving and jigging, I was physically relieved and spiritually released. Whether the pain was masked or actually banished, it was overcome by life and the fullness thereof.

We bobbed our heads as we passed reggae bands and hi-fived EuroCup fans as they strutted down the street singing victory. Sometimes we did a two-step through the dancing masses, and other times we just enjoyed them from across the street. But there were two parties we couldn't resist.

The first occurred in an alleyway, which is rarely the source of a good thing, but was also remarkably alluring. The sky had darkened, and our posse spread as we walked. Tom and I were up front, with Ben nearby. Luke prowled behind us, filming nonstop. Then there were Philip and Robbie, followed by an also-filming Mr. Hill. The alleyway was coming up on our left, deep, seemingly void of light and life. But there was a low pulse thumping under our feet, and we glanced around to find its source. The farther we went, the more the boom consumed us. Like a pool filling with water, the deafening heartbeat rose from our shoes to our chests and into our heads. As we passed the alleyway, the harmonic tumult reached its zenith and then, just as it rose, it began to subside. This is when we paused. Rather, Tom and I paused.

We bobbed our heads as we passed reggae bands
and hi-fived EuroCup fans as they strutted down
the street singing victory. Sometimes we did
a two-step through the dancing masses.

It should be noted here that Luke Thompson is a connoisseur of EDM (electronic dance music). He knows the names, the stats, the shows, all of it. And like a child to McDonald's, he is drawn to it from a mile away. So Tom and I paused, but Luke was already gone. With camera still running, Luke had made a left into the darkness and followed it into what we found for ourselves, just seconds after him.

While the mouth of the alleyway was pitch-black and empty, a few steps drew us into the throes of a Parisian rave. Folks were packed in wall to wall, and to one side a set of turntables and soundboards stood together with two DJs at the helm. Blue and green neon lights lit everything. Luke took in the scene, as did we. Strange. The music was a thunderstorm of sonic absurdity, and the crowd fit the bill in look but not in spirit. They stood around, lost and bored, in a sort of trance. We'd entered a dream world. A riddle with no answer.

I felt like I was in a Terry Gilliam movie. A mangy animal here, an abandoned bicycle there. Street urchins slipped through our legs in droves, and a misplaced neo-Nazi nodded hello. Truly, this was a place of unique environs and misfits. And it was hidden from us till we stepped into it. Had we passed through the looking glass? Would we find Alice and her Mad Hatter among these wacky, melodramatic patrons?

Philip came in after us, a rescue mission into the blue-green jungle of sloths and pandas. The lights and sounds were drowning us so that we needed guidance out. It took a bit more doing to retrieve Luke, and Philip went back in for him fearlessly, but we eventually found him and escaped the mysterious underworld.

We'd gone just a bit farther when we spotted a café (they're stereotypically everywhere in Paris). It was on the corner of an intersection, and where there normally set quaint tables and chairs on the sidewalk, we found another DJ with his soundboard and a crowd around him. They were anthemic songs, the kind you can't ignore—and unlike the alleyway rave, this crowd engaged fully.

We realized, as we approached, that our course would take us straight through the crowd, and we decided that was what we wanted. Tom sauntered into the middle of the group with me on his back and moves already in play. We were ushered in by everyone with cheers and rhythmic claps. The crowd noticed us as we entered and were all about it. The African worship circle had been comfortable with us, the ravers couldn't have cared less, but this—we were not just part of the shindig; we were the focus of joyous attention. We were rock stars on a Paris corner as we spun in circles, arms in the air, people moving with us to the thumping, happy tunes.

We were not just part of the shindig; we were the focus of joyous attention. We were rock stars on a Paris corner as we spun in circles, arms in the air, people moving with us to the thumping, happy tunes.

This was profoundly fun, and we stayed for a song before exiting the opposite side. After all, we understood the importance of getting out while we were ahead. We slid in as the life of the party and slipped out before that had a chance to change. Always leave them wanting more, right?

* * *

The team took on a low profile for a few blocks. We encountered gaggles of drunks, who invited us to this bar or that concert, and we kindly declined. It was fun when they'd realize our nationality.

Many of them were insistent on practicing their English with us, and amazingly enough, the farther gone they were, the better their English was.

Just a handful of blocks from our apartment, we came upon an old church. There was a crowd gathered outside, and a band was setting up to play (more akin to what I was expecting earlier at the African worship circle). We noticed folks going in and out of a church, so we decided to follow suit. A nice lady met us at the door with greetings and explained to us some of the church's history. The furniture on the inside was humble. Wooden chairs lined up before an ornate stage, surrounded by titanic pillars. On the outskirts of this layout, the walls were designed like miniature stalls. Within these stalls were relics, dating back hundreds—some of them thousands—of years.

As we entered, the band started up behind us. Great doors hung open to the public, so the music outside meandered its way inside with us. Tom was overwhelmed, pointing out, in awe, its harmony with the Gregorian dirge reverberating through the stone room. As one moved to minor, so the other moved back to major, the chorus, bridge, and so on, resonating keys and timbre to balance one another, by no means perfectly, but oh so full of grace. And all of this happened without either knowing the other. Two rivers, both deaf and blind, pouring into one mighty ocean.

We took a turn around the exhibit of relics and a little old woman joined us. I'm not sure of her connection to the church, but she knew its features like the back of her wrinkled hand. Her English was limited, but she showed us each relic with vigor and knowledge,

pulling us along proudly from one to the next. After this funny—
yet informative—tour, we thanked her and parted ways. The scene
was so tranquil, we lingered, and some even took seats for a bit.
Taking the moment to slow down in a peaceful setting allowed the
day's travel to catch up with us. Our well-deserved weariness set
in. This was when the little old lady returned, and she'd brought
friends.

"We have a statue of the Virgin Mary," one of them said (the
one who had greeted us at the door).

"Cool," we said, unsure of where this conversation would go.

They were clearly excited about this news, and we understood
the Catholic affinity for the mother of Christ. But why were they
telling us? Did they share this good news with everyone who
came through?

"It's behind the stage," she added.

"Okay," we said, carefully feigning excitement.

There was an awkward silence as they waited for something to
register. No such luck, so they finally said what they were thinking.

"We would like to take you back there," the nice lady said, "and
pray for you."

Still, it wasn't setting in.

"There have been many miracles to happen there," she added,
and that's when it clicked.

Now, I grew up in the South, where well-meaning charismatics
run amok. Countless are the times I've been offered healing prayer
or invited to healing services by friends and strangers alike. This
wouldn't necessarily catch me off guard or even bother me all that

much, except that this time I was without my wheelchair.

I had found that outside my wheelchair the world looked very different, and with that revelation, I expected the different-looking world to see me differently. But that wasn't the case.

For months, the focus had been on how cool it was that my friends were carrying me. That had been the miracle, not legs getting fixed. My disease had been overcome; it had been "cured" by my friends and me finding a way around it. No longer did it matter if I, or anyone else, was technically disabled. We'd proven that life could be lived regardless. That is a miracle. That is healing power. That is the kingdom of heaven. And yet here we stood in a fifteen-hundred-year-old sanctuary, being told it wasn't enough.

My heart sank a little. I gave a forced smile and pretended to think through their proposal. This is not a flattering recollection, justifying my actions or insisting I did what was best. I'm simply telling you what happened. I kindly accepted their invitation to see the statue but declined the offer of prayer, to which they agreed. Perhaps they perceived we were travelers in a strange place or maybe they thought we were unbelievers. Either way they did not mean to make us uncomfortable in their church. We followed them to the back of the holy room and stood reverently before the marble shrine. Our guides left us here, giving us time to ourselves.

The white stone woman was sweet and peaceful on her pedestal, a figure of comfort and grace, the pinnacle of motherhood, inviting to all and convicting to many. I had trouble looking at her, trying to balance the appreciated beauty of the place and the supernatural expectations that came with it. I felt her, like the women who'd just left us, waiting and hoping for me to change my mind. I even found myself waiting, hoping, wondering what could happen.

This brings me sadness, when my heart leans into this state, when my focus is distracted, moving me away from matters of the heart and lingering instead on the body. I lose sight of the wonder-working power the Creator of everything pours so freely into my life, and my world becomes small as I look down at my feeble limbs. Rather than dwelling on the goodness of my Father (what we were created to do in the first place!), I wallow in what is trivially wrong with me.

The focus had been on how cool it was that my friends were carrying me. That had been the miracle, not legs getting fixed. My disease had been overcome; it had been "cured" by my friends and me finding a way around it.

We remained there for a moment longer, in respectful observance of the Virgin, then moved on. Our time in the church had come to an end, we felt, but as we headed for the door, people began to flood in. It had started raining. The ever-serving Robbie went to help bring in chairs and band gear. Seeing that we weren't going anywhere for a while, Tom set me down and Philip sat on the floor with me. This is when our little old lady returned.

Shuffling up to Philip and me, she bent down to be as much on my level as she could. Her smile was optimistic as she opened her hand to present me with a gift. It was a small candle, featuring a portrait of Mary and a Bible verse about believing. This was her prayer, she said in broken English. Her prayer was that I believe. She used motions and her limited vocabulary, but soon grew frustrated. She wasn't conveying well enough, she thought, the weight of her prayer. I nodded, understanding, but she insisted on finding a translator.

As she ran off to find help, Tom and Ben joined us on the floor, admiring the gift. I was silent. I couldn't speak, couldn't do anything. This is how my anger is expressed—I shut down. The guys noticed my discomfort but didn't know why, nor the depth of it.

"That lady who showed us around," Philip explained to the others. "She gave this to Kevan and was trying to say something. She just went to find a translator."

"I wonder what she was trying to say," they mused together, but I answered quick and trembling.

"I know exactly what she's trying to say," I mumbled. "I've heard it a hundred times before."

They looked at me, realizing now how upset I was. I took a deep breath and continued.

"She wishes I'd have enough faith to be healed."

I watched as my words settled into my friends' minds and hearts, and confusion, sadness, sympathy appeared on their faces.

"Can we please leave?" I asked.

"Yeah, man," Philip said, getting to his feet.

"Like, before she comes back," I added, and they all nodded.

Ben gathered the others while Tom helped Philip strap in to carry me. In seconds, I was up and we had the gang together, heading for the door. The little old lady intercepted us with her translator friend (the greeter), who was clearly as uncomfortable as we were with the woman's persistence. The guys were great, protecting me from further harassment. As she approached, we simply waved, said a polite good-bye, and continued on our way.

I was silent. I couldn't speak, couldn't do anything.
This is how my anger is expressed—
I shut down.

Outside, rain poured down like a shower, an attempt of heaven to wash away the night's debauchery. There was a Metro entrance just across the street, so we opted for the short way home. The guys were worn out. I was spent. A few stops on the Metro got us to our neighborhood. The Place de Clichy monument greeted us like an archangel as we emerged from the Metro station and headed to our home around the corner.

* * *

My thoughts passed over the night with what I wanted to be an open hand. I reflected on the dichotomies: the African worshipers and the welcoming dance party, the Virgin Mary and her devout keepers. I reflected on three worlds: a fallen creation, the redeemed church, and my own silly heart. I reflected on Christ: his healing power, his saving grace, his love for me.

As we rode the Metro, climbed the stairs, and walked those dirty, luminous streets home, I boxed with the Lord and clung to him for dear life all at the same time. His mercies are made new every morning, and I was reeling for that sunrise to come.

I reflected on three worlds: a fallen creation,
the redeemed church, and my own silly heart.
I reflected on Christ: his healing power,
his saving grace, his love for me.

Once we were back and I was settled into bed, Tom came in to visit. We had a chair by my bed, and the guys took turns coming in on different nights to talk. This was Tom's night, and we would proceed to explore music and the very deeps of life, the usual path of our conversations. But as he came in, he turned to the balcony window, which hung wide open. The rain had subsided and the celebrations outside carried on throughout the night.

"Do you want the window closed?" he asked.

"No," I said. "It makes me feel like I'm still a part of it all."

ROBBIE'S POINT OF VIEW

I wanted to dance to the music, but all I could do was watch Kevan and Philip. I was frozen from the smile on their faces and from the people around us in the square. That moment when the drums pounded and flutes flared, we all fell in love with each other, some whom we would never see again, but the deal was sealed—I would forever be a part of something that couldn't be explained.

PHILIP'S POINT OF VIEW

It is interesting to read Kevan's recollections of our trip, and to see how some experiences impacted him in much different ways than they did me, but I remember this dancing experience vividly. This is partly because the video footage put together by Luke and Mr. Hill looks so fantastic.

However, I was also pleased that I used French to ask one of the women in the crowd if it was a Christian group (which was obvious because they were singing worship songs), and she understood me and answered. My high school French teacher would have been pleased. Despite this, I probably wouldn't have joined the group in their dancing, but having Kevan on my back helped me to let my guard down. Without knowing it, he pushed me to connect with others in ways that I would not have otherwise done.

10

BAND OF GYPSIES

THE MORNING OF JUNE 23, I awoke to a sunny Paris outside my bedroom window. It beckoned me to come and stay awhile, to walk leisurely among her people along the canal and through her city streets. We had experienced the nightlife, the sidewalk cafés, the pastry shops, and they all called for our return that bright and lovely morn. There was an electricity in the air and my waking breath took it in, but it was not for Paris to hold us. Not today.

For most of our trip through Europe, my friends were as excited and invested in our activities as I was. Paris, London, the English countryside, and especially Skellig Michael—these were shared dreams we wished to fulfill together. But this day was for me, to go somewhere and be part of something to which the others had no great tie. They were loosely familiar with Django Reinhardt from me playing his music and sharing stories, but that was about it. I was humbled, then, by their willingness to take me on a day trip to visit his self-proclaimed hometown of Samois-sur-Seine. What's more, we would be attending a festival in his honor. The town would be peopled with musicians who'd dedicated their lives to the gypsy style Django had lived, played, and developed.

* * *

I first stumbled upon the name Django Reinhardt in high school. I grew up on old jazz music and have always loved the genre, so my brother introduced me to a movie from the '90s called *Swing Kids*. The story follows a group of teenagers in Germany at the start of WWII who rebel against the HJ (Hitler Youth) and growing Nazi regime by adopting American fads. They dress like American kids, use English slang, and dance their hearts out to swing music. As the narrative unfolds, the HJ infiltrate their gang, and the struggle to join or fight becomes a matter of life and death for all involved.

In the film, one of the main characters is Arvid, a gimp who plays guitar in the underground jazz scene. There comes a point when Arvid is attacked by members of the HJ, and one taunts, "See how you play now!" as he crushes the cripple's hand beneath his boot. Later, in the hospital, we find Arvid unwrapping his mangled fingers. He says with a glimmer of nervous hope, "He said I'd never play again, but he forgot about Djangoman."

Who was Djangoman? I wondered. This is an intriguing scene in its own right, but it struck me especially because of his mangled hand. My teen years were difficult as I watched my strength diminish more quickly than before. I had already lost the use of my right arm, and now my left hand was failing me a little more every day. My ring and pinky fingers were going limp, the same two that were unusable to Arvid and, apparently, this "Djangoman."

My teen years were difficult as I watched my strength diminish more quickly than before. I had already lost the use of my right arm, and now my left hand was failing me a little more every day.

As it turned out, Django Reinhardt was a Romany guitarist wandering around France at that time. He was a musical prodigy, the kind who played premier dance halls in Paris at the age of twelve. But in his early twenties, he was in an accident that rendered him disfigured, especially in his left hand. His ring and pinky fingers were useless. Music was his great passion in life, though, so rather than giving up, he used his genius to redesign conventional chord structures. It was a long and frustrating process, but he reemerged better and stronger than ever, and he's remembered now as one of the greatest guitarists of all time.

* * *

To prepare the team, we put on some of Django's successors while we showered and dressed for the day. We listened mainly to Angelo Debarre, who has made quite a name for himself in the genre. I secretly hoped to see him on the sidewalk that day, plucking away at his guitar wearing sunglasses with a cigarette nearby. Should such a moment actually come about, I wanted the crew to be ready and have some context. Unfortunately, we didn't see him, but his music was still a fine way to start the day.

Our journey to reach Samois-sur-Seine from our flat in Paris should have taken maybe an hour and a half. This, however, did not account for waiting time, getting lost, and taking some unnecessary scenic routes. We took the Metro from Montmartre to the train station where we had a lengthy respite. Then came the train ride, and we learned how to set me in the train seat while still in the pack. Robbie carried me on his back into the train car, then backed up to a bench and sat sideways, so that our backs were to the window. Once he was unstrapped, the guys turned the pack so that I faced forward. My feet came out of the stirrups and rested beneath me on the bench so that I looked like I was squatting.

It was a surreal experience to sit in the window and watch a wild and thriving city like Paris dissipate and cottages and open land appear. Forests raced by and fields of white and gold spanned like oceans far and wide. Occasionally a village or small town would make itself known and we'd slow at a station to pick up new passengers, then we'd move again into the open fields, hills running alongside us in the distance like children at play. It was a perfect setting to process what was to come of the day.

When we arrived in Fontainebleau (the nearest station to Samois-sur-Seine), we discovered the festival had been moved due to flooding. The day was hot and sunny, but recent rains had caused the water to overflow the riverbanks by Samois and forced the town to evacuate. The news came to us in broken translations as we initially sought out directions to where we thought the festival would be. So then it was a matter of finding the new location, which was somewhere in Fontainebleau, but the last-minute change in combination with language barriers made specific directions difficult to acquire. We took a bus around the town—literally all the way around the town—and ended up back at the station with more questions than before.

It was in this whirlwind of weary confusion that we met Paula, the embodiment of Italian spunk and beauty. She couldn't have been more than five feet tall, with dark eyes, curly black hair, and a smile like the rising sun. Philip and Tom happened upon her in the train station while the rest of us waited under a bus stop shelter outside. Paula had overheard their attempts to make sense of when and where to find the festival, and she stepped in to help with her broken English. Our two friends came running back to us across the parking lot, and this glowing Italian lady ran with them, her guitar case swinging madly at her side.

Everyone introduced themselves, along with another guy who'd just come in from Sweden. He had arrived on the next train and was also confused about the location of the festival he'd come so far to see. Christof was his name. Paula took us all under her wing and gave us the rundown of exactly what was going on. She was a veteran of the festival and knew the ins and outs, even with the chaotic situation with the flood. She explained that the festival was starting that night at a castle in Fontainebleau.

As she described the concerts, her smile grew ever broader and she sighed contentedly as she recalled magical memories of previous years. Then she returned to us in the present and leaned forward with a secret. While the festival is great, she said, she was more excited about the campground where everyone would be staying. People were hanging out there, playing music together until the festival started. That's where she was headed. I knew enough about the festival and the Django culture to know this campground was the real jackpot, the heart of Django, and where we really wanted to end up.

"You can come with me if you want," she offered, and we gave a definite yes.

We had some time now, waiting for the bus. Paula got antsy. All this talk of Django Reinhardt, his music and followers, made her itch to play. Her foot started tapping as we looked out for the bus. Her fingers started tapping too as we paced the small spot of shade. Finally, glancing around with a harrumph, she sat down on a bench and took her guitar from its case.

"Usually," she said with a laugh, "the minute I get my guitar out to play, that's when whatever I'm waiting on shows up. We'll see."

She tuned the instrument and then asked me if I had a favorite Django song. Now, I do have a few favorites, but I'm not picky. The man's catalogue is unending, and it's all amazing. Also, to my shame, I'm not very good with recalling song titles. But most importantly, this was the first time I'd ever had a conversation with a fellow Django Reinhardt fan—someone who not only knew of him but loved his life and music. And she was asking me for my favorite song. A crippling nervousness came over me. My mind went blank. I shrugged, though I was smiling uncontrollably. I was in heaven and had no idea what to do.

Paula, gracious as she was to our weird little group, offered a title.

"How about 'After You've Gone'?" she asked. I nodded carefully. *Do I know this one? Probably. Who am I? What am I doing here?*

While the festival is great, she said, she was more excited about the campground where everyone would be staying. People were hanging out there, playing music together until the festival started.

She began strumming slowly, finding her pace. She nodded in time with the song coming forth. Then, under the bus stop shelter of a hot parking lot in France, Paula began to sing. It was sweet and strong, rich with vibrato like the jazz singers of old. After a few bars of lackadaisical swing, the feisty woman erupted into the choppy rhythms synonymous with the gypsy sounds of Django. Her eyebrows cocked playfully as she belted out the lyrics to a song from a world long gone, and I was there with her. Never had I heard these oh-so-familiar songs played in person, and with such heart, but now I was transported back to the 1930s, to a campfire by the Seine or a club in Paris. It made no difference where, the music rang with tripping, skipping life. History and the present smashed together in this in-between realm where time stands still, save for the tapping of its toes to the transcendent tunes.

I don't remember whether she reached the end of her song before our bus arrived. By the time I had my wits back about me, we were aboard and halfway to our destination. The campers, who usually set up in Samois, had moved downriver about two miles to Samoreau, on a thin stretch of grassy bank between Forét de Fontainebleau and the Seine. We reached this place in what seemed like a matter of minutes, and the bus pulled up to a clearing by the river. As the bus came to a halt and we filed off, I took it in—first through the windows, then outside.

Before us ran the Seine River, no longer held by bricks and boats, like in Paris, but swifting by wild and free as the day it was born. And to our right, stretching out to the far tree line, were tents and trailers raised. Tarps had been hung; chairs were strewn; there were barbecue grills set up and coolers of beer. And within this little ramshackle burb loafed a populace of gypsies, all singing and playing instruments together.

At the "entrance," if there could be one to consider, was a covered shelter. It was filled with tables and chairs, and a bar that served food and cold drinks. Like the campground, this area, too, was peopled with gypsies and music. The sun, somehow hotter out here in the countryside, seared our skin so that as we stepped off the bus, we made a beeline for the shelter. It had been a long day of travel and we were tired, hungry, thirsty.

Christof went his own way, as did Paula, though we ended up in the same vicinity. The guys found a table in the shelter, and we set ourselves down. I was on the floor, facing a circle of players whom Paula now joined. It was nice to begin the foreign experience

110

with what was now a familiar face and voice. In this small collection, there were three guitars and a fiddle. Paula brought a fourth guitar and her voice to the happy mix. Then one of the guitarists left. Another song, and someone else joined in halfway through. This, as we learned quickly, was the way of things here. Whether it was a Django move or a mannerism he simply picked up from his people, I don't know, but it was the understood structure of our present society. Think of it as a cocktail party or cookout, where folks mingle from cluster to cluster. No one is offended, interrupted, or surprised. It's just a constant flow of unique players dipping in and out of the numerous musical conversations.

Tom went ambling off to find a good spot to swim. The other guys collected around me, but here is my confession: I wanted to be by myself. For all the loving service poured out on me, especially that day—the long travel, the stress these men bore to carry me, their calm resolve and glad willingness to sort out our confusion—after all of that, my selfish heart wanted to be left alone here. I would struggle with this peculiar feeling a few times over the course of our trip, but this was the first. It stemmed from a desire to wander off on my own, to disappear into the crowd and process the experience without any influence of my friends around me. And at this point in the trip, I didn't know how to deal with that desire. I didn't even really know what it was, so I let it take the form of frustration. But again, my friends were gracious.

While I've known Philip and Tom the longest, I felt the most comfortable with Ben, simply because of our time together over the past few years. I had confessed to him that morning that I was struggling with a bad mood. So, after a few songs, I turned to Philip and Robbie and laid it out for them.

"I promise I'm not mad at you guys," I said, "but I really just need to go for a walk by myself, and I feel like the closest I can get to doing that is with Ben."

They both understood, and Ben strapped me on for a stroll through the campground. As we were about to part ways, Tom returned with good news. He'd found a watering hole, prime for swimming, and the others decided to join him. Before leaving, we turned to look out over the river. A smile was on Tom's face.

"You do realize," he said in a giddy sort of tone, "that Roman soldiers walked along this bank! Right where we are!"

I patted him on the shoulder and nodded. Django Reinhardt had lived along this river in the early 1900s, tickling fish and playing his guitar. But the historical relevance of where we stood ran so much deeper than a mere hundred years. Tom has always been good at drawing the romance out of a place or situation, and I appreciated his enthusiasm as he took my precious view to a broader, more profound level.

Tom went off to join the others at the watering hole, and Ben and I headed into the folds of a gypsy campground. Luke and Mr. Hill followed us with cameras rolling, which drew some attention, but not nearly as much as I'd expected. We were as far from mainstream anything as I think one can get, buried in the basement of subculture, and these folks prefer to keep it that way. So I wondered how the musicians would respond to a film crew. As we approached groups mid-song, they'd glance up (sometimes) and just keep play-ing. Perhaps they were comfortable with it, or maybe they held to the idea that if you ignore something, it'll go away. Whatever the case, Luke and Mr. Hill never had issue. Only one man even acknowledged them, an upright bassist in his late forties. Between songs, after a terrific solo on his part, he pointed to Luke with a furrowed brow.

"Did you talk to my agent?" he asked sharply, still pointing his fat finger at our friend.

"Oh yeah," Luke replied with a goofy grin. "He said we're good."

A moment of tension hung as everyone looked on. The man's calloused face loosened to a grin, and the collective broke out in laughter. We, too, gave in to laughter and another song started up.

This was the extent of our verbal interactions with the residents. In the sheltered bar, folks were kind enough to move chairs or clear an area for us to sit. The strange sight of us (this gang of rednecks carrying a cripple around on their backs) did prove disarming any-where we went in Europe, and the gypsies were no different. They weren't necessarily talkative or even inviting, but amiable enough for us to linger with little, if any, discomfort. We were clearly out-siders, but no one seemed to mind. In one way or another, everyone here was an outsider.

---

*The strange sight of us . . . did prove disarming anywhere
we went in Europe, and the gypsies were no different.*

As we joined circles of music, I felt like a kid coming to watch his big brother play video games, squirming to stay cool and quiet while his hero doesn't seem to notice. And just like that kid with his big brother, I was ebullient there in their midst. They were all so laid-back, reclined in lawn chairs, their instruments loose in their arms. Fingers flicked at strings and danced smoothly along the guitars' necks. Ease and pleasure are the signs of mastery. And this was how they spoke: with music. Sometimes a glance or nod would signal solos, and sometimes melodies would be hummed to recall a song, but mostly folks just listened well to each other. Familiarity lent itself to this, the songs played being classic jazz standards and Django's style the common dialect.

These pockets of artistry were comprised of two to ten players, with folks floating in and out at random. And ages ranged from single digits to last legs, all masters of their instruments and fans (even students) of one another. Fathers, sons, grandfathers, daughters, and mothers sat in circles and built together a resonant framework to showcase each other's skills.

It was a lot of fun, and as Ben and I walked along, listening to them play by the river, I realized more fully than ever the character of Django and his music. Playful and lazy, free as the river. I was challenged by these folks' memories of the man—they dressed and groomed themselves like him; they spoke his language and played his music. But they didn't limit their playing to two fingers, as he was forced to do, and they didn't sit around marveling at his courage or strength to succeed despite his impairments. They played his music and adopted his tenaciously wild heart into their own able-bodied lives. It was not because he overcame disabilities that they were inspired. The spirit itself with which he overcame inspired them, and that will live on as a legacy from generation to generation.

How do I live my life? The question begged to be asked. By what do I strive to be known and what of me will be remembered? Will I inspire those around me because I am a strong man or because I am a strong disabled man? One of these will last longer than the other. One is deeper. Identity is key. While some of this is contingent on others' perceptions, how I'm remembered also leans heavily on my conveyance. May my heart, in the Lord's good keeping, beat stronger and louder than my feeble limbs and spastic neck. When I am long dead and gone, may my love for life and others be what resonates. When friends recall me to memory, may they recognize me for my laughter and the look in my eye, and not the chair I'm sitting in.

Since first hearing his name and learning his story more than fifteen years ago, since first his music knitted itself into my soul, I have been inspired by Django Reinhardt. He has provided the soundtrack to many of my struggles and victories over the years. And I don't know if we would be friends, but I do know we share a deep strength. Django was a wanderer and a fighter, a man full of life. My interaction with his people left me thinking we could sit without a word and enjoy life together along the river. Him playing his guitar and me scratching down stories, or both of us just sitting in silence watching the day go by from under a tree.

As Ben and I wandered around the camp, I could've sworn I

saw the gypsy himself leaning against a tree with a cigarette on his lip. I heard his tattered, whimsical fingers along the old strings of every guitar. I saw his mystic gaze in the eyes of every patron. And I felt his restless, unbreakable heart beating in my chest.

* * *

I was recently reminiscing with Tom about this day we spent by the Seine, and we were surprised to find we referred to the day in two different ways. I referred to it as "The Django Day" and he called it "The Swimming Hole Day." We knew we were talking about the same thing, but our subconscious associations of it were entirely different. If Tom, or many of the other guys, wrote a book about our trip, this section would be about traveling to a campground and skinny-dipping in the Seine River all afternoon. I like to think the tone would be akin to that of *The Adventures of Tom Sawyer* and send you back into childhood for a few minutes as you swam and played with my silly friends on a hot summer day.

While most of our team stood waist-deep in the cool water, enjoying the sun's dance on its ever-breaking surface, Ben and I sat under the shelter and enjoyed a final bit of music. This was when I realized how much like the river Django's music really was. Most genres swell and bend together to build a smooth world of sound, one in which we wade and surf and dive deep. But these notes tripped and skipped, rippled and fiddled among each other. You can't sway to it, or even tap the straight beat. No, you fall into it; you flick your ankles and wrists to it; you let it carry you, but it'll take you up in ways an ocean never will. It's untamable, but not in a mighty stallion kind of way, more like a quirky squirrel kind of way. Even the slow songs have a nervous energy to them that leaves you unsettled until you hear it by the river and it all makes sense. The river moves along at a steady clip in its entirety, but its waves have a mind of their own within the boundaries of the whole. It's unsettling until you let go and give in to what it is. It's a river, not an ocean, and certainly not land. You give in to its spastic rhythms and moods, and you find it playful and restful all at the same time, like Django, his life, his music.

Most genres swell and bend together to build
a smooth world of sound, one in which we wade and surf
and dive deep. But these notes tripped and skipped,
rippled and fiddled among each other.

Ben bought us chips—a pile of piping-hot French fries wrapped up in a wad of tinfoil. We added ketchup and mayonnaise on the side and dove in. I had forgotten to eat for most of the day. The band that gathered under the shelter numbered a loose dozen, and the song they played never seemed to end. It was a grand finale, I think, a perfect ending to our day here in this wayfaring world.

I was so lost in the river jig enveloping me that, before I knew it, we were halfway through our chips, but Ben was suddenly balling them up to throw them away. With a single word and a subtle point of a finger, he made clear why my long-awaited meal was going the way of the buffalo. The area was crowded, and just beside us sat a gentleman and his cigarette, ashes drifting our way and settling as seasoning on our chips. Maybe it was the spirit of the day, the people, the music, the river, or maybe I was just delusional from hunger and heat, but those ashes didn't really bother me. In fact, they befit the motif, didn't they? I had to smirk—a gypsy sort of smirk—at the proverbial icing added to our cake.

* * *

As we rode the train back into Paris that evening, I watched as a countryside relinquished its beauty to the industrial world and then folded itself into cityscape. And as we climbed the stairs to reach our flat in Montmartre, I reflected on the campground experience.

Because of my friends, their abilities and love for me, I was able to live like Django Reinhardt for a day. I walked where he walked, sat where he sat, enjoyed his river alongside his people, and we lost ourselves in his legacy, the music of his heart. I loved every second of it, but I also felt a strange thing—a longing, a homesickness I couldn't explain. This place, this society, was a kind of utopia, but there was something missing. I wondered at it under the shelter, listening to the last songs, and I thought about it on my way back, all the way to bed. The next morning I sat by the window in my room, looking out toward Sacré-Coeur and reading my Bible. That homesick feeling still lingered, and it led me to the tail end of Isaiah 55, where he shares his vision of the Kingdom Come.

"You shall go out in joy and be led forth in peace; the mountains before you shall break out in song, and all the trees shall clap their hands. Instead of the thorn shall come up the cypress; instead of the brier shall come up the myrtle; and they shall make a name for the Lord, an everlasting sign that shall not be cut off."

This is a promise from the Great Creator, the King of everything. He's laying out what exactly he has in store for us, and Isaiah describes, earlier in this thought, a world of provision and life. "Come, all who thirst, and drink water; beggars, come buy with money you don't have, buy and eat! Lean into me; hear me, that your soul may have life!"

And as amazing as we can imagine it, try as we may to mimic it here, he says we won't even come close. "As high as the heavens are above the earth, so my ways are higher than your ways." So we settle for glimpses now, slivers breaking through the old door of heaven and shining out on this side of eternity. Glimpses of the promise. Glimpses like this gypsy camp.

I can't argue one way or another for the souls along the Seine River, whether they know Jesus or even care. But I know I saw a kind of rest there, and I saw a kind of unity, a harmony akin to what we'll find among our brothers and sisters in heaven. We'll know all the songs; we'll know them to our very core. They'll run in our veins and out from our lips and fingers and the ends of our toes. And we'll contribute together, unique, and yet as one in love with the source and breathing this rhythm. And the songs will be old as time—and time will by then have died of old age—yet every note will be new and fresh, never heard before, and this will go on forever as we join the choir of hills and trees, declaring the name of the Lord.

Yes, I was homesick. I still am. It's a subtle ache in every beating heart, a feeling that something is missing. You know it too, don't you? It's always there, and glimpses like this, at what is to come, tenderize the aching so that we feel it more, and sometimes it's overwhelming.

I sat that next morning by my window, alone with a promise from the Great Creator. I wept for home as the vision of it settled into my chest, Isaiah's description overlaying the memory of the day before. I was homesick, my soul was homesick, not for Carolina and not for Fort Wayne, but for heaven, for streets of gold and a sun that never sets, when and where all is made right, when this ache will finally be quenched and we may know what it means to be whole.

Come quickly, Lord. Come quickly, please.

MR. HILL'S POINT OF VIEW

I blindly followed Kevan and his team of friends throughout Europe, seeing sights I never expected to see. Leaving Paris and heading south, I had no idea what beauty awaited, both in scenery and culture. I captured everything in time-lapse, and this was the perfect day for it, with blue skies and soft white clouds.

The people accepted Kevan and his entourage of film crew as if we were all family. I watched Kevan soaking up the sounds of the never-ending music while rubbing elbows with the best musicians around. Kevan was bold and adventurous, inspiring me to live a little more in the moment. As I filmed him dancing to the rhythms in the air, I didn't hold back to tap my foot a little . . . behind the cameras, of course.

11

CROSSING
THE CHANNEL

WE WERE EXPERTS OF PARIS by our final night there. That's what we thought, anyway.

We spent the day gallivanting around town like we owned the place. Luke had gone out earlier that morning to explore and invited us to join him a few blocks from our flat, on the rooftop deck of a mall. On our way, we stopped at a sweets shop, where we stocked up on chocolate, marzipan, and brandied cherries. It's a highlight of life, to sit on a roof in Paris, with the whole city in sunny view, eating brandied cherries with your best friends.

After this, we ventured back to where it all began. It seemed fitting to return to Sacré-Coeur. We explored the cathedral and enjoyed its steps for a bit before heading back for an early night. There was packing to do, laundry, and an early morning at the train station. We set our alarms to allow plenty of time and had everything ready to go. The plan was foolproof, tight as a drum.

When we woke, we hopped a few subways, which we could do in our sleep by now, and rolled into the train station right on time. Thirty minutes to relax before getting on our train to London. We set down our bags while Tom checked the boards to make sure the train was as on time as we were. I was on Philip's back, and we were debating whether or not to set me down for a bit. We had time, right? Tom studied the board, our tickets in his hand. He glanced down at the tickets, back at the board, then at the tickets again. A look of dumbfounded horror came over his face, and we all knew before he said it. We had messed up.

"Philip," he said. "Can you look at this?"

Philip took the tickets and confirmed Tom's fear.

"Oh my gosh," Philip said slowly, and Tom threw his head back.

"How," he asked, "how did we miss this?"

"I don't know," Philip said, equally dumbfounded.

Without another word, they began collecting bags.

"What's going on?" we asked, and the truth came like a wake-up call.

We, the experts of Paris, were at the wrong station.

At thirty years old, I have done a great many things, but I have never run. This trip of ours was meant to bring me into new experiences, but I hadn't expected this one.

We've all seen it happen in movies. George Clooney and his

chain gang jump onto a moving train to escape the wardens and their dogs; Val Kilmer runs across campus in his infamous "Eureka!" moment of 1985; Jim Carrey, God bless him, races through an airport to rescue his love's briefcase. Now it was our turn. We had thirty minutes to reach the other station in Paris, all the way across town.

At thirty years old, I have done a great many things, but I have never run. This trip of ours was meant to bring me into new experiences, but I hadn't expected this one.

We ran—and somehow Philip and I were out front. Comfort and security were the least of our concerns as we descended one set of escalators and scaled another. I bounced this way and that, unsure of how to handle this new sensation. I thought of *Highlander* and Sean Connery's words of wisdom: "Follow the stag!" Just go limp and fall into the movement, like our dance during the Summer Solstice earlier that week. Running is like dancing, or maybe it's the other way around. Either way, I clenched my teeth (so as to not bite my tongue off) and went rag doll for the ride.

Our gang hopped barriers, bought passes, and somehow stayed together as we jumped from one subway to another. At one point we lost Ben, whose pass was a dud. Someone went back for him, and the rest of us waited at the approaching subway car.

It slowed.

Still no Ben.

It came to a stop.

No Ben.

The doors opened.

Ben came into view on the stairs!

He would never make it in time, so we resolved to wait for the next one. But Luke didn't get that memo and threw himself into the car. The doors began to close behind him and he turned around, realizing we weren't with him. Instinct kicked in. He struck his hand and foot out to stop the doors—but such doors cannot be stopped. They closed ruthlessly, and he had barely reclaimed his limbs before the train shot off into the dark. He signaled that he'd wait for us at the next stop, and we caught up to him then.

Another few stops, which felt like an eternity, and we reached the right station. Somehow we had five minutes to spare. One more set of stairs and we found a clerk, who greeted us . . . but told us we were too late to check in. Cutoff was thirty minutes prior to departure. Plus, Brexit had gone through the day before, causing all kinds of security issues. It was hopelessly out of our control. We'd have to buy tickets for the next train. It wasn't in the budget, but we had no choice.

Tom headed to the ticket office, and I suggested to Philip that we follow. It couldn't hurt, could it? I will admit, my intention was to pull the "cripple card" and see if we could catch some kind of break.

Lo and behold, it worked!

The man behind the counter heard us out, and while we offered to pay the exorbitant transfer fees, he kindly dismissed them. Soon we were going through security and boarding a train to London.

Once on the train, we met our respite with open arms. I think we all found sleep on that ride, as well as a few new friends. One, a man named John, was on his way home after coming to Paris for the EuroCup. He proudly hailed from the Welsh town of Llanfairpwllgwyngyllgogerychwyrndrobwllllantysiliogogogoch. We had him repeat the name a few times, and he was happy to do so. We told him about our adventures, and he invited us to visit him. Unfortunately, we couldn't on this trip, but hopefully in the future, which I'm sure he will hold us to. I hope so, anyway. Maybe once I've learned to pronounce the town's name.

One more set of stairs and we found a clerk,
who greeted us . . . but told us we were too late to check in.
Cutoff was thirty minutes prior to departure.

The United Kingdom hospitality continued as we arrived at our stop in a small town just outside of London. We were greeted by our host, Mike, a jolly man with long features and a bright shirt. He carried us home in his town car, and it took no time at all to feel comfortable in his flat. His girlfriend, Claire, joined me in their living room to hear about our journey so far. She was an adventurer herself, I learned, having been a competitive rower and cyclist until she was diagnosed the previous year with multiple sclerosis. The year had taken a pretty rough turn for her and Mike as she quickly became more and more limited in her strength and stamina. Our lives were an encouragement to her, as was hers to me, and we enjoyed each other's stories.

When we first started gaining media attention, around March or April, we'd received countless invitations to stay with people in the countries we were visiting. We were even invited to countries we weren't visiting.

Most of these invitations were kindly declined for one reason or another, but Mike's caught our interest for two reasons. First, he said our story hit home for him, due to Claire's recent diagnosis. Second, after inviting us to stay with them, he added the caveat, "We do live out in the country, which may be less appealing to you if you're wanting more of the city experience."

I wrote back, "The country is exactly where we want to be!"

After dinner, some of the guys went to bed, and I was headed that way. But Mike pointed out that Glastonbury, a huge music festival in England, was on TV that night, featuring that year's headliner live. So I joined him, along with Tom and Ben, in the den to watch Coldplay and their audience light up the night sky. It had been a long day, a day of racing hearts and close calls. I wouldn't exchange it for the world, I decided, and I wouldn't have it ending any other way.

TOM'S POINT OF VIEW

The story is this—we bought the tickets at that train station. I only assumed we would be leaving from the same station where we purchased the tickets. Amateur move, I know. Let that be a lesson for ya.

12

IN SEARCH OF THE BOY WHO NEVER GROWS UP

THERE IS A MAP OF LONDON, drawn by J. M. Barrie, which I keep in the back pocket of my mind. He drew it when he was still a young man and making plans to take the city by storm. His loving mother worried about him and his dreams of being a writer. He would starve or go crazy, certainly, she thought. She worried most about him leaving their humble Scottish town to live in the belly of a beast. To sooth her anxieties, Barrie drew the map and walked his mother through the world he would soon inhabit.

"Here's Big Ben," he pointed out, "and here's where the Queen lives. We'll have tea now and again. The post office, the Gardens, and there's the library, of course."

How accurate it was didn't matter for its purposes—he left out Hyde Park altogether. To Barrie and to his loving mother, this was London, and they strolled together through the make-believe world with rich autonomy. He had studied maps and photos, read all he could on the place and admired resident poets from afar, but the great city was still a mystery to be discovered in person one day. And yet, the unknown swayed him so little, it was as if this city were his own doing all along and he'd been there a hundred times over. Before he even set foot in it, James Matthew Barrie was a favored son of London, England, and he had the map to prove it.

As we awoke the morning of June 27, we rubbed our eyes, grabbed a snack, and boarded a train from Oxted to Victoria. Time collapsed onto itself as the English-speaking world flew by in a blur outside my window, and I unfolded the map to study it for myself. I fought back a strange nervousness, a tremor in my chest, like hunger but a little higher up. I had not known Paris in the least, and all of Ireland would be the same, but London—this bore a wholly different weight. This was where my literary giants trod, where they breathed in their tobacco and jotted the words that have beat and cut me into who I am today. The man who was sitting on that train was their doing, and the city I was racing toward was responsible for those men.

They say when G. K. Chesterton stood from these train seats, two women could fill his spot. The infamous Arthur Conan Doyle walked down Baker Street and said, "Yes, that's the place!" And Sir J. M. Barrie sat by the Long Water and decided a garden's as good a place as any for a baby to hide. Yes, I was on my way to a place otherworldly, and I had no idea what I was getting into. Just as John Donne asked for Christ's heart of submission in the garden, so I hoped for Barrie's heart of courage in the city. The old author sat down beside me on that train, leaned in with his funny little mustache, and pointed out to me the places on his map, feeding my soul and my imagination, walking me through the world I would soon inhabit.

London . . . was where my literary giants trod,
where they breathed in their tobacco and jotted the words
that have beat and cut me into who I am today.

"Here's Big Ben," he mumbled with a finger hovering over the paper, "and here's where the Queen lives. You'll have tea now and again. The post office, the Gardens, and there's the library, of course."

* * *

For the previous few years I had worked for a podcast company. The staff were spread across the world, and I saw my visit to England as a chance to meet a few in person. One coworker in particular was my friend Lauren Morse, who lived on the southern coast of England. She was the brains behind our rendezvous and schedule for the day in London. She also acted as a sort of guide for the day, and she did a wonderful job. But when we found her in Victoria Station, Lauren was deliberating intently on what sandwich to get from WHSmith's—cheese ploughman's or ham and tomato.

Our gang had just come into Victoria Station the day before, so we knew where to go to meet Lauren. That was the easy part, finding the right room, but there were three tricks to the situation. First, I was the only one who knew what she looked like. Second, as foreigners, our phones' capabilities were limited, so we couldn't just call her. And third, Lauren is short—very short. So off the train we went, and our team agreed on a spot to reconvene. I was on Robbie's back, so he and I went looking for her while the others found food. Luke came with us, faithful to capture every moment on camera.

We made a circle around the great sea of transients. No luck. No Lauren.

Something I came to enjoy as the guys carried me throughout the trip was that I was a head above whoever carried me. I was always at least tall, if not abnormally tall. I could see for miles, no hips or book bags in my way, no dodging swinging arms in crowds or guessing people by their belt buckles. I could see faces, all the faces, and they could see mine. But as we scanned the world of the busy station, no luck, no Lauren.

Something I came to enjoy as the guys carried me
throughout the trip was that I was a head above
whoever carried me. If not abnormally tall. I
could see for miles, no hips or book bags in my way,
no dodging swinging arms in crowds
or guessing people by their belt buckles.

"A'ight! What am I lookin' for?" asked Robbie, glancing left and right as he walked. "What does she look like?" He is a focused man, driven by his mission.

"I dunno," I said, racking my brain while scanning the room. "She's . . . a girl . . ." I hate multitasking. "She's an animator, kinda nerdy, so probably colorful. Skater, so . . . I dunno." I now realize I could have just shown him and the other guys a photo. Hindsight is 20/20, isn't it?

Another lap around the ever-commuting crowd. Worker bees and salmon pushing forward. All of us on the move. We passed a post, and something caught the corner of my eye. *I've seen that shirt before.* But a split second and it was gone. Did I even see it? And its wearer had her back to me, so I could've sworn it was her but . . . was it? I went with my gut.

"Go back, go back, go back!" I cried, and Robbie spun around.

There she was, standing in WHSmith's, studying sandwiches. Bright shirt, bright backpack, Chuck Taylor's. I didn't even have to say anything. Robbie knew, and so did Luke. We startled her, I'm sad to say, and derailed her near-decision on a sandwich. Despite this offense, she was thrilled to see us, and we made introductions all around. Once we found the rest of the group, the game was on.

First up, we would catch up with some other podcast folks at the British Museum. This meant taking the Underground, which proved much easier with a native, though she moved quicker than we were used to. While our gang spent minutes decoding maps and signs, Lauren deciphered them at a mere glance. She was also unfettered by the accent (as it was her own) and registered conductor announcements easier than breathing. Under her competent direction, and with my absolute lack of need to watch my step, I had the delight of reading signs as we went from one stop to another. Piccadilly, Paddington, Wimbledon, Waterloo, and of course, King's Cross. Mythical places I'd heard of, read about in books, and seen in films and television growing up, but now I (and hundreds of others) passed through them as casually as one might pass through Dayton, Ohio.

While our gang spent minutes decoding maps and signs, Lauren deciphered them at a mere glance. She was also unfettered by the accent (as it was her own) and registered conductor announcements easier than breathing.

And just as casually, we came to the gates of the British Museum, a massive construct of class and resolve. We entered the courtyard and took an immediate left to endure security (a trial for our film crew every time). Luke gained access, passing as a common photographer, though our dear Mr. Hill was held back for his excess gear. He attempted some covert filming in the courtyard while we were inside, which led to his being escorted off the premises. We didn't know this until we found him pacing the sidewalk a few hours later.

In the museum Philip carried me as we descended the stairs into the South African hall. It was a joy for me to have this experience with him, to glean from his contagious excitement. Folks have asked me what it's like to be carried. "Is it a symbiotic exchange?"

they've asked in jest, but it is, in fact, just that. With time, the carrier and I grow to share a kind of identity, like fighter pilots or synchronized divers. Our desires and reactions to the world around us meld into something new, and we each experience that melding as a give-and-take process. In this case, Philip had studied extensively the history of African cultures and longed to see some of the artifacts in person that he'd only heard of or read about in text books. Like my desire to be in the hills of England, my friend wanted to walk the halls of this museum and take it all in firsthand. And just as my experience in the countryside became his own by proxy, so this precious moment for him became mine as well.

Our steps were slow as we made our way through the rooms of artifacts. Tools, weapons, dishes, and ornaments, hand-crafted and hundreds of years old. Massive costumes, woven rugs, even etchings. Everything had a story, and it all came together to tell the tale of lives, generations, worlds otherwise lost in the winds of time. One of our favorite displays was one of ivory vessels, carved with beautiful designs in unbelievable detail. Philip, and so I, too, approached each glass case with religious stillness. We stretched high and knelt low to see everything, and Philip read aloud some of the descriptions, out of pure wonder. Others he relayed to me and anyone around us, giddy to share his joy and interest. I found myself caught up in his fascination and was thankful to be with him for this part of our journey.

We were accompanied by Lauren, as I mentioned before, as well as a few students. One of them, Hannah, remained with us throughout the day, much to our delight. She was quiet, to be sure, but pleasant company, and I must salute her and Lauren for putting up with us as we trekked all over the city. We were also met for a bit by Anne-Marie, a gentle American lady who'd married an Englishman some years prior. And finally, there was Amy, whom I remember particularly by her sketches in the museum. As the rest of us roamed the rooms of artifacts and discussed our findings, I noticed Amy lingering contentedly before certain displays, her sketchbook open and her pencil at work. A sculpture here, a piece of pottery there. Gray lines, quick shades, casting these images in her own hand.

As we came out of the hall, we stopped by the esteemed Rosetta Stone to pay our respects. Then it was onward to meet up with Mr. Hill and Tom (who'd set out on his own). Upon our exit from the building, we realized we'd lost a few of our number, so we waited for them on the steps. Philip set me down to rest until we were all together again and ready to go. It was lunchtime and the courtyard had filled with school groups and local business folks coming to picnic on the lawn or relax at the outdoor café. We grew peckish and decided our next stop would be for food. Lauren retrieved her phone to work out the route.

"Here we are," she said, kneeling down to show me. "And here's Kensington. We can grab some sandwiches from across the street and eat in the park."

We noticed then (and by we, I really mean the ever-thoughtful Lauren) that we were just a short walk from the Great Ormond Street Children's Hospital. She pointed it out to me, knowing my admiration for Barrie, who supported the hospital in his day.

"We can swing by on the way, if you'd like," she said.

My heart stopped. Lunch was suddenly not so important to me, and the glow of my face made it obvious. I remember trying to downplay it, screwing up my eyes and saying something like, "If we can just stop in for a second." But no amount of twisting could mask my smile.

We were just a short walk from the Great Ormond Street Children's Hospital. She pointed it out to me, knowing my admiration for Barrie, who supported the hospital in his day.

Our crew reconvened, and Robbie strapped me on for the next turn of walking. The hospital was a couple of streets away, and Mr. Hill caught up with us on the way. It spanned at least a block, so that we rounded a corner to find the older wing of redbrick and black hinges. Farther along, the structure evolved into a newer fashion (still brick), and tucked between the two ages was a covered walkway leading to a pair of silent, sliding doors: the visitors' entrance. We stopped at the mouth of the walkway and read the white words over the far-off doors: "Great Ormond Street Hospital For Children." Then the colorful word *Welcome* came into view as the doors slid open.

Do you recall the opening scene to *Raiders of the Lost Ark*? (Of course you do!) Indiana Jones steps carefully, reverently, awe-struck and trembling, toward the idol. You can measure every foot placement and hear the ancient grit give beneath his boots as he moves closer, sweat-framed eyes locked on the prize before him. You're holding your breath. You're gripping the armchair with blanching knuckles.

Robbie stepped carefully, reverently, awe-struck and trembling, down the covered walkway toward the entrance. Well, he walked carefully at least—the rest was on my part, my sweat-framed eyes locked on the prize before us. What a sight we must have been to those coming and going: parents worrying for sons, brothers praying for sisters, nurses serving wards and relieving one another. And here we were, my friends and I, come to stand at their doors like Moses on holy ground before the burning bush.

As we reached the doors, they slid open, beckoning us, but my focus was just to the left, and we turned there to find a garden box. It was maybe five feet by five feet with wild vines winding through a mess of friendly flowers. At the center, a bronze boy with shaggy hair crept suspiciously by, leaves crossing his lap like a kilt. His right hand rested open at his chin as he blew a handful of fairy dust upon all who passed in and out of the hospital. His left hand stretched up behind him, fingers spread to accept a fairy perched there lightly. And at the base of it all, a plaque shimmered, commemorating Sir J. M. Barrie for "his gift of Peter Pan to Great Ormond Street Hospital for Children."

In 1904, Barrie released the play *Peter Pan* and then the novel in 1911. Both enjoyed uncanny success, and in 1927, he signed the rights over to the hospital. Another plaque reads, "In remembrance of J. M. Barrie, who, by the gift of his Peter Pan to help sick children and by many other kindnesses, proved himself a true friend and generous benefactor to this hospital." It wasn't enough that he was chairman of the board or that he blessed them with financial gifts. Barrie also did for the children there what he did for the rest of the world—he gave them hope. I find it interesting that the various memorials to him around the hospital refer to his "gift of Peter Pan," as in not just the copyright, but more so the person, the idea, the symbol. He gave to those halls the spirit of a boy who wouldn't grow up. And the boy still runs wild through the rooms, playing hide-and-seek with angels; howling with pride; laughing at life, death, and everything in between. . . .

Another plaque reads, "In remembrance of J. M. Barrie, who, by the gift of his Peter Pan to help sick children and by many other kindnesses, proved himself a true friend and generous benefactor to this hospital."

A child is admitted, sick and scared, covered in blankets. Her mother, also scared and covered in blankets, sits by her bed with heavy eyes that eventually close to sleep. And in the dark of night, the child and her fever are visited by the boy as he perches himself at her feet. Baby teeth shine as he smiles. She asks his favorite question:

"Who are you?"

Oh, he loves to talk about himself!

"I'm youth. I'm joy," Peter answers. "I'm a little bird that has broken out of the egg."

He sees the red in her face and the tears in her eyes. It is curious to him, and he cocks his head to say so. She is afraid; he knows no fear. She is sick; he can fly. She ages before him with every sniffle; he will never grow old. And one day she may be the mother sitting by this bed, just as her sleeping mother once was the child. Peter Pan will be forgotten to her by then, merely a bedtime story, nothing more, but tonight he is perched at her feet with a dangerous grin. And whether or not he knows, or is forethinking enough to even care, he is there to make sure she lives to be that mother.

Death prowls near like a lion. It slinks along the hall and slips into the fevered girl's room, wet nose sniffing her out. Peter presses a finger to his lips and shushes the child as he leaps down from her bed. He unsheathes the blade at his side and strikes it dramatically on the laminate floor. Then, rising to float, he cuts a circle around himself and the bed. His grin spreads wider. There's only one thing he loves more than himself, and that's a good fight. Death stands at the edge of the circle and glares up at the boy. The boy glares back, blade ready.

"Cross it," he whispers to Death, "I dare you."

Courage. Strength. Joy. The stuff of survival.

J. M. Barrie gave to the children a fighting chance. He gave them a figure their size, to hold their hand in the night as monitors beep beside them and blood is drawn by cold needles. While the grown-ups use words bigger than the ocean, Peter says low in the children's ears, "Come away, come away!" and plays his panpipe till they dream.

"His gift of Peter Pan" will last longer than any money Barrie could give or fame he could accumulate. The author loved people and that love has outlived him, spanning generations with the eternal youth of a boy and his shadow. As I stood before that statue—the bronze boy watching, his cheeks threatening me with flight—I was overcome with the weight of a legacy. Who am I living for and what am I leaving behind as I go?

"His gift of Peter Pan" will last longer than any money Barrie could give or fame he could accumulate.
The author loved people and that love has outlived him, spanning generations with the eternal youth of a boy and his shadow.

I've read several of Barrie's novels, and also the speeches he made and letters he wrote. A master of wordplay, a wizard of stories, the man was whimsical and profound, a smitten weaver at the loom of language. And he used his creativity to encourage others, to speak life and draw it from the deeps of his audience, strangers and friends alike. This came not with ease, but with struggle and hardship. His boy Peter cries, "To die will be an awfully big adventure," and Barrie wrote the line with his brother, his mother, and his friend Mrs. Davies in mind. "I want always to be a little boy and to have fun," Peter declared, as Barrie himself longed for a lost innocence in the fallen world. The theme shows up in everything he wrote, but into the tales of Peter Pan he poured it all without holding back.

This is the legacy he left behind, to every mother, to every child—his heart and hope for something better. It challenged me to examine myself, my own creative efforts, and what their ends might look like. He gave away so freely his most prized character, because I believe he knew the good of it was bigger than he could ever be, as I would see later that day in Kensington Gardens.

*　*　*

Before the publication of the play and novel, Peter Pan took his form in another medium. In 1902, Barrie commissioned a famous sculptor to build a statue of the boy and place it in Kensington. It would be set, ten years later, in the exact spot where Peter landed after flying from his nursery window to escape his mother's plans of law school and government seats.

How appropriate, after our sweet morning together, that Philip should carry me to the foot of the old statue. I was humbled by his care as we circled it in silence. Earlier in the day he'd drawn me into his passions at the museum, but now our roles were reversed as my wonder took over and I began to share stories from the book and the legends around it. Philip listened attentively and took me for another turn around the statue.

While the hospital's boy stalked with hunched back and darkness in his eyes, the garden's stood tall with puffed-out chest and flute held high. He played a song, and it drew to his feet fairies, critters, and mothers, climbing black rock to reach their tragic hero with a touch. But who can touch Peter Pan? I reached out my hand and ran it along the rock, over the mothers' shoulders, and considered two great things.

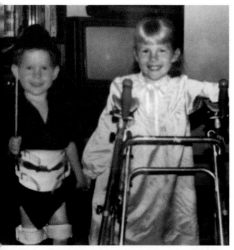

Halloween 1989—me and my sister, Connie, as Peter Pan and Wendy.

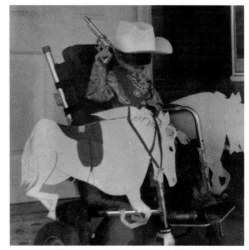

Halloween 1990, me as the Lone Ranger (my brother drew the horses).

My brother, Andrew, reading to me (1991).

Third grade soccer at school.

Behind the wheel on my parents' driveway in NC (1990), with my brother and Dad.

My band and full-time job through high school and college, Fluffy Road-kill, with best mates Danny Stapp and Zach Lycans.

Greensboro, 2014, first ever backpack—me and Tom ready for the sewers.

Greensboro sewers—Philip, me, Tom.

My sister, Connie, and me (2011) on the BC ferry headed to Victoria.

Sean Wang making espresso with me at Fortezza, 2016.

Testing a backpack early on in Fort Wayne—me, Ben, Tom, and Philip.

My first test run in the backpack in Greensboro, 2016.

Paris—"we made it!"

Into the belly of the beast.

Chillin' by the Eiffel Tower.

Atop *Sacré Couer.*

Royal Albert Hall 2016—Ben, me, Philip, Tom, Robbie.

Looking out over Paris.

Kensington, Peter Pan statue
commissioned by Barrie himself.

Kensington.

Westerham after our long hike—
Ben, Tom, me, Mike Pocock, Philip
and Winston Churchill

Climbing up
Skellig.

On our way down Skellig.

On the pier of Holyhead, Wales.

Mexican dinner in wales—
Luke, Ben, me, Robbie, Philip, Tom.

Chapter House, 2017—
me, Andrew Peterson, and Ben.

Fort Wayne, 2017—with my brother,
Andrew; sister-in-law, Amanda;
sister, Connie; mom and dad.

Great Wall, 2018—Marcus, me, Tom.

Luoyang, Chi

Luoyang, China, with Nate Renich,
Marcus, Phil Shay, Tom.

Me, Ben, Lauren in London, when I travel
to Ireland to give a TEDx Talk in 201

The first was that J. M. Barrie loved this boy and believed in him so much to say, "Let's give him a statue" before anyone else really cared. He'd shown up in some of Barrie's writings already, though nothing like his grand premiere two years later. But he knew this clever character was different from any of his others, different from anything the world had seen before. You don't build a statue to the mundane and common, but to world-changers, and so Peter was.

And second, I stood in that place and realized that the author himself had stood there a hundred years prior and approved this very sight before me. I was looking at the Peter that Barrie saw, and this was a sort of comfort to me as a creator. We live in a culture of stories rendered beyond recognition. Works created once with passion are altered, reimagined, and deconstructed until one has to ask, "Why didn't we just make something new in the first place?" It seems the demand is that everything be fresh and fit into the pop culture frame, whatever the cost, and even the Boy Who Never Grows Up is no exception. It's discouraging to writers like myself who fear Hollywood's influence upon our precious worlds. So to see this pure depiction of such a beloved creation was refreshing and encouraging, and I took it in like a breath.

We live in a culture of stories rendered beyond recognition. Works created once with passion are altered, reimagined, and deconstructed until one has to ask, "Why didn't we just make something new in the first place?"

This statue, and the great garden around it, brought me back to my thoughts on creative legacy. Thoughts of a writer wading through a world soaked in entertainment. What am I building? And what will the world do with it? Will it be remembered? And why? At thirty years old, I should have a family, a normal job, some sense of stability, right? The pressures settled in; loneliness and doubt rolled over. The old author sauntered up alongside me then as I stood shivering in June. His funny little mustache twitched with a grin. His hands were tucked away into pockets, and he rocked on his heels like a bottle.

"You'll be all right," he said casually, his Scottish lilt rolling.

I stared at the statue, reflecting on the ups and downs of Barrie's life, and I knew he had as little idea of what he was doing then as I do now. But he stayed faithful to what he knew—loving people and telling stories—and trusted the rest would work itself out.

"Kevan," and he said again, "you'll be all right."

The Lord agreed, and I believed them both.

* * *

I've jumped ahead. A few things happened between the two Peter Pan statues: more of the Underground, lunch, and a news interview, as well as visiting a few other statues. Two memories, though, should be noted.

There is in Kensington Gardens, not far from the palace, a pond rightfully called Round Pond. Folks lounge here on the lawn, sit on park benches, and romp playing games in the late-afternoon sun. And we walked through, enjoying the summer rest that hung like a dream over the land. But the dream was broken by the curses and laughter of a group of boys at the water's edge. Maybe a half dozen of them ran along in a gaggle, one of them carrying an inner tube and rope. We got closer and found them taking turns tossing the inner tube as far as they could into the water.

Splash.

Curses.

Pull it back with the rope and try again.

They'd lost their soccer ball to the pond and it bobbed, frustratingly, just out of reach. Two older women sat on a bench nearby and giggled at the trials of youth. We had to join them. It was too comical to turn away. Tom—who had rejoined us on our way to the park—considered helping, having a better understanding than they of aerodynamics, but we held him back. Don't ruin our fun, Tom! I think they would have turned him down anyway. They enjoyed the struggle and the attention.

Splash.

Curses.

Pull it back and try again.

The splash would send out a wake that bobbed the ball closer. Rejoicing! Then the next splash would knock it away. Back and forth it went, teasing the boys and tickling us to no end. Finally, the wakes were favorable, and the ball came in to be caught. One of the boys scooped it up as we all cheered. And not a moment later, another took it from his arms and tossed it back onto the water. Curses and laughter. Soccer was fine, but this would be their game tonight. We chuckled and moved on.

Farther along, just around the corner from Peter Pan, we came upon a clearing full of birds—pigeons, to be exact, and a flock of bright-green parakeets. They swooped and soared, hopped and fluttered, always pecking and diving for seeds. Yes, there were seeds! Seeds galore, thrown and held (and eaten too) by an elderly man with no voice. He was stocky, square even, and slow in his movements. His gray hair was tussled, his mustache unkempt, and his clothing hung loose on his shoulders so that the mystery of where he began and ended might remain just that—mysterious. He stood with feet spread, limbs wide, head back, and birds alighted on him as if he were a great tree for nesting. In his open hands, upon his head, and across his shoulders sat piles of seeds, dinner for the green beauties, and he rejected their ugly brothers with a wave of his hands.

Lauren stepped in first to join him, and Hannah was close behind. The man filled their hands with seeds and ours too. He then went back to standing still and we mimicked his stance. Pigeons collected around our feet, and parakeets wove overhead like streaks of green ribbon. They especially loved Tom, who accepted them with sovereignty on his outstretched arms.

The old man came wordlessly to Philip and me, and he sprinkled a mound of seeds onto Philip's head. He smiled with his eyes as he stepped back and the birds began to come. I was quickly visited by the rear of a parakeet, its feathered tail flicking at my nose. It finished the feed, and when it returned later to rummage for scraps, it met me face-to-face. We stared each other down until we had a silent understanding, then it burst into a violent flapping and took off. Another came later to nibble at my ear—which the other never would have done; we had, after all, an understanding. I saw his soul and he saw mine, and when that happens, you don't try to eat one another.

The next morning we had breakfast with our hosts, Mike and Claire, and mentioned the parakeets to them. They laughed when we asked about them. Is the garden a preservation of some sort? No, Mike explained. Some thirty years ago, a handful of them escaped from a pet shop, and wild breeding has led to thousands settling around the Kensington area.

We came upon a clearing full of birds—pigeons, to be exact, and a flock of bright-green parakeets. They swooped and soared, hopped and fluttered, always pecking and diving for seeds.

There's something fitting about this. It's sort of whimsical and romantic that such an elegant bird should decide its home would be among fairies and runaway babies. I can't help but recall Barrie's secret—how appropriate it is here—that children, "having been birds before they were human, they are naturally a little wild during the first few weeks, and very itchy at the shoulders, where their wings used to be."

As we left Kensington Gardens, my friends and I chatted and laughed and debated our route back to the train. The sun was setting on the parakeets' trees, and I took in deep breaths of the world around me. I was inspired, aware, and restless. I felt the Lord laying foundations for new stories in my heart. I felt an army of fairies watching me from the darkening brush. They waited eagerly (and perhaps perturbed) for our departure so their evening's revelry could begin. Reality is a beautiful thing, but I also felt the weight and joy that it will never be enough, not as long as there's imagination and a kingdom coming. As we left Kensington Gardens that day, I felt my shoulders itching, and I hope to God they never stop.

LAUREN'S POINT OF VIEW

Never had I met a group quite like this. I was busily choosing sandwiches in London Victoria Train Station, waiting for Kevan and crew to arrive, when out of the corner of my eye an oddly tall shape loomed into view and called my name. I turned to be faced with Kevan, seven feet up, and a bunch of strangers I'd never met.

After excited introductions and hellos, working our way through streams of commuters to the Tube, my instinctual London pace was quickly checked by my new companions' easy stride. Something told me the schedule would not fall neatly into London's busy heartbeat . . . and that this day would be wonderful. To be in the presence of such an uncommon group—woven together by self-sacrificing, honoring love—wakes you up and shakes off the dust from your soul. And this whole-hearted embodiment of love and kindness truly has the power to change.

In our parakeet-filled moment, standing spread out, in near silence, marveling at these bright gems, and smiling and laughing to each other as they alighted on us, I suddenly understood the impact of this true love and honest kindness. It's not how you'd always expect—it catches you by surprise. You don't realize you've been hit by it until afterward, like an unexpected gift.

I thought Kevan was just inviting me along to catch up and meet his friends. What he actually invited me into was a gift so powerful, and so gentle—that of truly grasping what it is to love one another, and the unexpected life and exuberance it creates.

13

INTO THE
ENGLISH WILD

THERE ARE KEYHOLES IN LIFE through which technology just won't
fit, no matter how hard it tries. It can climb into your hand and
hang on tight, it can nip at your heels so you don't forget it on your
way out the door, it can get plenty of sleep and exercise so it's ready
to go, but there are experiences that can only be truly captured by
the present human senses, and in those rare occasions, cameras,
microphones, cell phones—none of them stand a chance. History
is made up of these moments, these keyholes, and they are held
forever afterward by the oldest medium in the world—man's God-
given memory.

On June 30, we left behind civilization by way of a Westerham
alley and set off into the English countryside.

As is typical for the UK, we had no idea what the weather would look like, but it seemed to our host as good a day as any to go for a walk. When he's not biking cross-country or making friends with everyone he meets, Mike volunteers with the National Trust. Once a week, he pitches in to clean up and preserve the protected grounds behind his house. Woods, fields, pastures—some marked with trails, some rimmed with fences, some as natural as the day God said, "Let there be . . ." All of it hung like a portrait out the window of Mike and Claire's lovely home, and all of it was available for our free roaming.

Foreseeing our course, Mike made sure our day started with a proper English breakfast. He took us down into Oxted, to a local café, where he introduced us to cups of tea. These were swiftly followed by plates piled high with the heartiest of sausage links, beans, ham, assorted vegetables, toast, poached eggs, and, of course, blood pudding. Let it be stated that I, for one, enjoyed the blood pudding, though (to be fair) I still don't fully know what it is, and I plan to keep it that way. Ignorance is bliss, especially when you can cover it with HP Sauce.

Mike was grinning ear to ear as we got our fill of his favorite traditional English meal, and the waitstaff loved our rowdy crew of ragamuffins who had invaded their usually quiet town. This was our fifth day in Oxted and word of our presence had spread, so everyone recognized us and greeted our team jovially. I think it had less to do with us and more to do with Mike's rapport with the community. As we walked down the road with him, everyone said hello, and he'd return the greeting with their name and a warm handshake. When we'd be out on our own, the townsfolk would refer to us fondly as "Mike's friends." In time, we came to call our host the godfather of Oxted, with all of his connections and well-earned respect. If we brought this up, Mike would just laugh and shake his head, but can't you see Brando or DeNiro giving the same humble response?

Let it be stated that I, for one, enjoyed the blood pudding, though (to be fair) I still don't fully know what it is, and I plan to keep it that way.

After breakfast, some of our number parted ways for the day. Mr. Hill headed into London to collect some b-roll footage, and Robbie enjoyed a day of video games at the house. The rest of us piled into Mike's car and drove over to Westerham, just a few miles down the road. We could have walked it any other day, he explained, but we had enough walking ahead of us.

* * *

When we were making arrangements with Mike while we were still in the States, he had listed some of the sites around their house that we could see on day trips, and one was Chartwell, the home of Sir Winston Churchill. I have a profound respect and curiosity for the historical giant, a love that runs deep in my family's bones, so visiting Chartwell was a must.

Mike had our route all worked out: a looped walk that would

take us out of the hamlet Westerham, up around Chartwell, and back down into Westerham. Hamlets are neat little towns where business and living blend subtly through one another to make up a charming cluster of community. It would be about a six-mile hike total, claiming the better part of an afternoon.

* * *

Mike parked the car and we suited up, Ben taking the first turn carrying me. We walked in a line, with Mike up front, and as we turned down an alleyway, the pubs and shops evolved into cottages with picket fences and wild trestles. Each home had a name (get your act together, America), and we embraced the enchantment of their unique personalities: Ravensbrook, Greenhelm, Shirewood, and so on. Soon the houses grew sparse and were replaced with brush and trees. The picket fences became barbed wire, and wide-open fields came into view.

Our path was awkwardly narrow for the first 150 yards, a steep ascent with wire and branch guarding our entrance into the freedom ahead of us. Imagine a tunnel of foliage and difficulty, and as we climbed, a distant light promising repose. Mike is a brazen trekker, so as he tromped along, all of nature was swept aside by his sturdy frame. We did our best to keep up, and he called back, "Almost there! It'll open up in just a minute."

The night before, as Ben carried me home from downtown, we got lost and marched uphill through the wrong neighborhood. Now he found himself carrying me uphill again with no end in sight. He began to wonder if there was some sort of conspiracy against him. "I feel like I'm getting the short end of the stick here," he said, pausing to catch his breath.

Philip took up the pack then, relieving Ben after the short but rough walk. Once Philip and I were set, our team turned to see the hamlet below us. We took in the expanse hanging behind Westerham. The little town was great to look back on, but it was only a speck on the living map before us. Hills of green and gold rolled lazily under the weight of a blue sky. Thin clouds strolled by, and villages speckled the horizon.

A world unbelievable rose up around us, and a favorite revelation came to me in that moment: nothing was out of reach. We were in the middle of it all and going farther in. My whole life—whether from a highway, in a movie theater, or on my parents' front porch—I'd looked out on the unattainable heights and depths of this world. I could've been looking at the moon or Atlantis, it was all so out of reach. I'd never be there, not really, and I came to terms with that a long time ago. My imagination would have to suffice, but when I see open fields, my heart still reaches for them like a child. My compulsion is to run straight for them with complete abandon. Before the trip, I shared this idea with Tom.

A world unbelievable rose up around us,
and a favorite revelation came to me
in that moment: nothing was out of reach.
We were in the middle of it all and going farther in.

"If I were able-bodied," I told him once as we drove through the Midwest, "I'd pull my car off the highway and just take off on foot into those fields."

"What would you do then?" he asked.

"I'd get to the middle and I'd stand there. That's it. Just stand, by myself, out in the open of opens. No interference, no distraction, just the field around me and the sky above. I think then, maybe—just maybe—I could finally feel free. I could breathe deep, calm my heart, clear my head."

I'd imagined it a thousand times: the run through a field, the walk through a wood, standing out amid the color green. I'd looked upon those far-off worlds and stretched my mind past breaking to set myself there. And now, here we were. It wasn't my imagination. This was real life in full swing, and I was a part of it.

As amazing as the sight was to us, even to Mike, we knew there would be more, so we followed our fearless leader. We came to the end of our fence and crossed it to walk along the edge of a wood. There was something akin to a path, I guess, but it became evident to us that Mike just knew where to go. As we walked, Tom's prone-to-wander sensibilities were tempted, spotting gaps that led deeper into the dark wood.

"What's in there?" he'd ask, and Mike would passively say, "Oh, just another path."

I can see it now, and I have to laugh. Tom, like a curious toddler, shifting his feet, leaning off the beaten path. He'll never leave us, but his steps sway, and that strain of his neck; he yearns to explore. Stay with us, Tom. We'll get there, I'm sure.

Reflecting on the fence we passed through, Mike told us about the government's recent effort to make such things more handicap accessible. Up until a few years ago, fences on the countryside had stiles—a step that allowed practical up-and-over passage. And this worked for hundreds of years. But the powers that be decided this was a hindrance to some and a change needed to be made. Their answer? You will find retractable, circular gates on the more modern fences, which cuts out the difficulty of climbing over, but brings its own issues. In order to pass through, you push the door open as you step into the circle-pin, step to the side, swing the door back, and step around it to exit out the other end. Yes, it's as frustrating as it sounds. And besides being grounded, it's no more accessible than the stile. We got a good laugh out of wondering whom they were trying to accommodate.

The first fence we crossed was this new-and-improved version, and let it be noted the difficulty we had with it. Can you see it now: a grown man trying to fit through a circular maze-stall with another grown man strapped to his back? But our next fence was yet to be updated. Philip and I approached warily. Correction. I was wary. Philip was perfectly fine. While this was an entirely new experience for me (hopping a fence), Philip had hiked, climbed, and backpacked, and I'm sure he'd hopped a few fences in his life. Once again—I think it was at least once a day—I had to forfeit my preconceived notions of what was possible and trust the experience and wherewithal of my friends.

But that's really high up, Philip! And it's a thin, rickety step with not much to hold on to. And you're top heavy, and . . .

We were up and over, just like that. I wish I could say I was good to go after that first one, but it took a few more stiles before I was really comfortable.

After that first stile, we took a turn into those woods Tom so badly wished to enter. The temperature dropped as we ducked into the canopy, and a chill ran across my shoulders. It might have been the shade that caused it, but maybe it was also the mysticism of the place. The greens and golds of outside faded to darker tones with a coat of gray. Shafts of light streaked through to add a sort of gray web over the scene. As we walked, I looked around at the trees, from their roots to the branches above. They stood bold with inveterate life, hunchbacked and gnarled but stronger with every passing day. I felt protected, somehow, by their looming, knotted boughs, and the chill in my shoulders ran deeper as we strolled through their ancient courts.

This is where lore becomes a reality. Walking through such a wood, shrouded in magical history, Robin Hood seems suddenly practical and King Arthur a part of the furniture.

As an aside, here's something I'm amazed by: the natural coordination of able-bodied feet. It's as if they have a mind of their own. When driving my wheelchair, I make myself aware (or am rudely made aware) of every bump and divot I cross. But as I was carried through the wildwood by men with functional legs, I noticed their feet working independently, unconsciously, to navigate the uneven terrain with ease. In short, there was significantly less tripping than I expected.

Throughout our travels, it was a running half joke that

everything was merely a buildup for our final climb; it was all training for our ascent of Skellig Michael. When difficult moments arose in our day-to-day, the guys would write them off as preparation for the big hike. It was mostly brought up for laughs, to help us get through, but there was some level of truth to it because we were intentional about each guy having that experience. And it was Philip's turn. We approached a steep climb, similar to Ben's but muddier and shadowed. I remember looking up at the ascent and saying to myself, "Oh boy." Philip, too, was hesitant at first, but we both let out a deep sigh and mustered our resolve.

This is where lore becomes a reality. Walking through
such a wood, shrouded in magical history,
Robin Hood seems suddenly practical
and King Arthur a part of the furniture.

Tom went before us, and Ben behind. And the trees stayed close on either side, available for us to brace ourselves against. When Philip and his feet could find a root, it would give him purchase and he'd rise with a grunt. Sometimes, though, his footing would find no root, but only mud. It was a struggle to make any progress. Still, Philip is persistent and strong, so our climb was slow but steady, and after many grunts and great strides, we arrived at the plateau.

We soon came to open fields again and were greeted by cattle. They lounged in the tall grass. Straw hung from their fat lips like cigarettes, and they nodded lazily to us as we passed. Somewhere amid the cows, we switched carriers, Tom taking his place in the rotation.

It was in this open space that we realized our lack of technology. Tom had left his phone at the house, and Philip pulled out his camera to use, but to no avail—it was with us in body, but its spirit was long gone.

Ben's spirit began to wane as well, along with his body. His allergies decided that this of all days was the one to make themselves at home in his face and chest. In all fairness, we sort of opened the door and invited them in when we set foot in the countryside. His eyes swelled and wept. His sinuses filled, and his breathing became labored. Ben, though, is the toughest mug I've ever known, and he is faithful to the grueling end. His endurance is Jason Bourne level. The guy will push through anything. So, even though his allergies had kicked in, he stayed with us as a backup carrier.

The cow pasture led us along the edge of the wood we'd just emerged from and eventually funneled us back into the trees. Before reentering, however, we had a chance to spot a number of estate houses in the distance. All were old, but as is the case with people, some carried their age majestically while others looked hollow and haunted. Should we go that way and get close enough to peer in? But we continued our route without tarrying. Once back within the trees, Tom discovered his challenge for the day—an incline similar to the one Philip had endured.

"This won't be the last either," Mike said apologetically. "There's a worse one yet to come."

Tom nodded, preparing his calves and his mind for what lay

ahead. This is something I appreciate about Tom: he internalizes the storm and then heads into it. It may take a minute to process what he's about to take on, but he never says, "No thanks." He nodded again and began the climb.

I faced another difficulty on the guys' backs that day: branches overhead. Sometimes the limbs droop a little low, and my friends would be forced to bend at the knees to dodge their prying fingers. On Tom's back, this proved an even greater issue as those branches overhead were no longer so overhead anymore. His height, even at a ducking stoop, put me face-to-face with leafy talons and razor-sharp greenery that struck without warning or prejudice. We made it through all right, but more than once I feared for my eyes and imagined my forehead was probably streaked with cuts. This was an aspect of the hike I had not foreseen and do not look back on fondly, but this is the way of hiking—discomforts are part of the experience and must be taken together with the beauty and joy. Obstacles, whether internal or external, enrich adventure and deepen the profundity of a journey.

Tom discovered his challenge for the day—
an incline similar to the one Philip had endured.
"This won't be the last either," Mike said apologetically.
"There's a worse one yet to come."

As we went, our weaving in and out of woods became frequent, and we found a few roads as well. Philip and Tom switched another time or two, reserving our dwindling Ben as a last resort. All the while, Mike led with a smile and an endless yarn of history alongside childhood memories. He'd grown up in the area, after all, and so had his father.

As promised, Mike took us by Chartwell, and this led us into further conversations of history. Mike is, as he would put it, "a bit of a military nut," so we really got the inside scoop. We didn't just have a local on our side, but one who knew what he was talking about and articulated it well. As we stood before the wall surrounding Winston Churchill's home, we enjoyed its modesty—modest for being the home of a prime minister, at least. Though it was big and obviously the house of wealthy folk, it was by no means a castle or mansion. There were certainly more grandiose homes in the area. We appreciated this and believed it said a great deal of Churchill and his family.

Of course, these days the house is not in private use but has been converted into a museum. This costs money, and there was an old man at the gate to make sure the toll was paid. As plump and sweatered as he was, the look in his eye and the cane in his hand suggested we not test his limits. We were on a budget, so we observed the place from outside, peering over the wall and through the gate as best we could, before moving along.

It was not long after this, back in the thick of trees, that Tom displayed our oneness of mind. Sometimes he notices things I would appreciate before I even pick up on them myself. Such was the case here. We were cutting cold shadows through the trees when Tom, with me on his back, suddenly stopped. Everyone else stopped around us. Mike, who was up front, paused and looked back. Such stops were common for adjustments or switch-offs—but Tom was in need of neither this time. His eyes creased as he peered into another world to our right.

"I think I'm channeling Kevan when I say we should take a brief detour," he said slowly.

As my muscles weaken over time, they also tighten in strange ways. My wrists turn inward, one of my legs won't straighten, and my neck can't turn to the right. So I had no idea what Tom was talking about until he turned so I could see. And there it was—an opening in the foliage. A radiance of green glowed from the opening and stretched into the darkness on rays of sun. It looked like a gateway into an oasis, a promised land. Tom led the way. We passed through and were met by a fence running parallel to our course. Beyond the fence sloped away a massive green field, and beyond the field rested a forest darker and more mystical than any we'd yet passed through. Everything around the place fell captive to the shadow of the brooding wood. So foreboding, even from so many miles away, it stood rich and terrible as a living, breathing giant.

"That's called the Weald," Mike said. "It's an ancient wood."

We remained here for a while, looking down at the ominous beauty of untamable nature. For all the old structures and age-tested cultures we had been part of over the past week and a half, this was something else entirely. This was creation, old as time, ordained by God and planted at the foundation of the world.

I wondered what stories could be told, how lives have been changed there under deep leaves; words and wars, love, life and death unfurling within those shadows over countless generations. What ghosts still linger? A kind of gravity pulsed from that mass of black trees, and it pressed against Tom and me so that we leaned on the fence for support. I felt small and strong, threatened and sheltered with my friends in the presence of such a place.

I wondered what stories could be told, how lives
have been changed there under deep leaves;
words and wars, love, life and death unfurling
within those shadows over countless generations.

A little ways farther, we were introduced once again, though briefly, to civilization. Cottages and mansions lay scattered over roads and gardens. One such home was being renovated, and Ben, still suffering from allergies, took advantage of their Porta Potty, purloining its toilet paper supply for his survival. He slipped the roll into his belt and used it to blow his nose for the remainder of the walk. It was among these houses, too, that Mike volunteered a turn at carrying me.

"I've got a bad knee from my college days," he warned, "so I don't know how long I can do it. But I'd like to try."

As you can probably guess by now, with what I've told you of Mike, he conquered a significant portion of the walk before deciding he'd had enough. He even handled some serious mud pits and a few intensely narrow steps in and out of a gorge. All the while, our conversation dove into his life and mine. There is a level of intimacy that comes with strapping a man to your back, a band of brotherhood, a communion that links you as one person. As a mother bears her child and they are one, so is a man carrying another on his back. The common struggle and united achievement, the interaction together with the world—there is a tethering that the experience produces and the outpouring of that is a sharing of each other's deepest self.

Mike had spoken before of Claire's multiple sclerosis diagnosis, but now he went into further detail. He pulled no punches as he let out its effects on his heart and their relationship. He opened up the doors of his past, his angels and demons alike. I listened and had the opportunity to share my heart as well, especially on disability— the struggles, pains, fears, and joys.

In every man's life there are moments that are especially profound, though they may often be subtle. A conversation at the grocer, a paragraph in a book, a hug from a friend—seemingly inconsequential, yet life-changing as we are built up, encouraged, reminded that we're not alone. This trip was full of such moments, and this was one of the greatest to me, one of the most dear.

And another cherished moment came soon after. Once again I was on Tom's back, and once again he "channeled Kevan." We were climbing a knoll, which turned out to be quite a foreboding hill. Once we reached the top, there was a fence to pass through and then a wide, verdant field sloping downward toward distant Westerham. Our loop was nearly complete. We were almost home. After a long day of hard walking, we could see the end, though it was still far off. As we stepped through the field, I noticed we followed a trail of pressed grass. It must have been the route taken by most who passed this way.

At the crest of the knoll—picture us now, looking down over the rim of the world—Tom paused and looked around.

"Yep," he said aloud, nodding. "This is good."

"Yeah, it is," I agreed. It was a glorious sight—but he meant more than that.

"Okay," he announced. "Guys, help me set Kevan down."

"Wait," I cried. "What?"

Ben and Philip came around to lift me while Tom explained. "We're going to set you here and leave you."

I stammered and stuttered. Leave me? Where were they going? I was suddenly sitting in the pack on the ground, grass rising over my feet and all around me. The tree lines and hill country spread out before me. The hamlet lay far below. The sky was blue and streaked with white overhead. Ben blew his nose. Philip rubbed his hands together (a habit of his). And Tom stretched his tired back.

"We'll be over by those trees," he said, pointing toward someplace behind me that I couldn't see. "I wanna sit on that fence."

"W-w-when will you be back?" I asked.

"In a bit," he said simply. "We're in a field, man. This is your chance."

The others agreed, and I was suddenly alone. By myself. In the open of opens. As my friends' voices trailed off behind me, I settled at last into the truth of where I was sitting, of what I was doing. And it might not have been my exact vision—running into a field and standing. That'll have to wait for the Kingdom Come. But I was in a field and I was alone. Let's call it a glimpse of heaven, because our Father gives us those now and again. It was this glimpse that inspired the giants who came before me too. As I sat there, I felt I was joining their table. I understood Barrie's childishness, Chesterton's wildness, Tolkien's enchantment, Lewis's clarity. Eric Liddell ran through these hills and knew God's pleasure.

It might not have been my exact vision—
running into a field and standing.
That'll have to wait for the Kingdom Come.
But I was in a field and I was alone.
Let's call it a glimpse of heaven, because
our Father gives us those now and again.

I took in a deep breath, scanning the horizon, the sky, and even the grass around me. I let my sight sink into the trees off to my left, and I watched the clouds like they were passersby on a city street. The hamlet lay tranquil, while beyond it the hills brimmed with centuries of life. And though they were still far off, as such places have been all my life, they were tangible now because I was among them, part of their existence. I was sitting atop one of their number and so I sat atop them all. And on this hillside, my heart calmed, my head cleared, and I finally felt free. I found freedom in a simple truth as it came over me like a blanket—the world, my

Father's world, is a big place, and I am part of it. And it was a freedom not like that of escapism but a step into strength, possibility, and wonder—the freedom to live a full and rich life anywhere, everywhere.

After maybe ten minutes (I'm guessing—it could have been an hour), Mike returned and sidled up next to me. He had his usual grin, his arms swinging as he glanced around with his whole body involved.

"You know," he said, pointing loosely to the sky, "this is where the Battle of Britain took place."

The others gathered together, and our host went on to describe the details: political dynamics between England and Germany, Hitler's promises to Chamberlain and Churchill's perception to the contrary, the Nazi onslaught on these English heavens and the Royal Air Force's mighty reply. The line of defense held and drove Hitler and his fighter planes back home, never to mess with England again. As Mike regaled us with the adventure, his chin rose high in pride for his country.

I couldn't help catching some of that pride, enjoying the mark of victory over evil. Looking back up at that old, blue battlefield, I could almost hear the dogfights roaring and spitting shells. I could see the planes ripping clouds apart, like knives cutting cotton, as they dove and twisted around each other in the heat of battle. The clouds, now some seventy years later, pass like the veterans of a battle move—like my own grandfathers move: old men triumphant, though battered and wounded still. There is wisdom in

that movement. Their heavy steps and wrinkled eyes are monu-
ments more profound than any statue or placard we can fashion,
and in those thunderous steps we may hear an echo of the greatness
required of once-brighter eyes and once-lighter feet. War's effect on
man and nature has more to teach us than any history book or film.
May we learn from its lasting impression and never forget.

* * *

Ben carried me on our descent back into Westerham. One more
sloping field and a cluster of woods ushered us back into town via
another alleyway. This one proved not so postcard as the last, and
Ben (struggling, but taking life like a champ) had to step up into
an old-but-very-much-in-use aqueduct system. The others were
able to nimbly step onto its ledge as they climbed over to safety
while keeping dry, but this would be an impossible feat with me
onboard. So my dear friend went faithfully—and wetly—forward,
and we found ourselves sitting comfortably in a pub five minutes
later. Pints all around for a hike well done and toasts to every man
for his valiance and strength.

As we left the pub that evening and headed to the car, we noticed
three things. First was the park, which boasted a small patch of
grass and a handsome statue of Churchill at its center. He was
reclining, as Mike explained the man had done often in that park.
There was also a statue of General Wolfe—the man credited with
securing Canada's subjection to Britain in their race with France
to claim it. And finally, as we parted ways with these two stone

figures, we passed an antiquated building: the George and Dragon. Without slowing our pace, for these are common sights to him, Mike leaned toward us and said with a chuckle, "Well, that pub is older than your country, isn't it?"

*　*　*

On July 2, the time came for us to leave England for our next destination. This was the final stretch of our journey, through Ireland to Skellig Michael off the west coast. We could have flown, but we hadn't gone anywhere by boat yet, which was an option this time. So we took a train to Holyhead, Wales, and from there, a ferry to Dublin.

We heard a great many terrible things about Holyhead before arriving there. Jon, our proud Welsh friend, had tried to sway us from going. "Come to my town instead," he said, describing Holyhead in terms I won't repeat. But then Mike used the same words, verbatim, when he heard where we were headed. Apparently this was the general consensus.

But it was the port for our desired ferry. We took the train from London and a few hours later found ourselves in a quiet and dilapidated costal town. We collected our things from the train and made our way through the empty streets to a bed-and-breakfast by the pier. Most of the buildings we passed were vacant, and many were boarded up. Holyhead, as best we could gather, was a ghost town.

On the way to find our lodging, we laughed at a restaurant whose sign boasted coffee and genuine Mexican food. Growing up in North Carolina, I was used to such a sight. There are taquerias on every corner in North Carolina and most southern states. But in Wales?

The bed-and-breakfast was quaint. It was even decorated with a garden out front. Our rooms on the second and third floor looked out over the water and a golden sunset. We unpacked and cleaned up from the day of travel. Some of the guys called home to check in on family. Then we reconvened to decide on dinner.

We laughed at a restaurant whose sign boasted coffee and genuine Mexican food. Growing up in North Carolina, I was used to such a sight. . . . But in Wales?

For all of our joking about the Mexican restaurant earlier, we retraced our steps to have dinner there. We entered the restaurant to find the combo on the sign made more sense—the main level was a coffee shop and upstairs was the restaurant. The gentleman hosting, named Jay, greeted us with a smile and led us upstairs to the dining area. A floor-to-ceiling mural of Butch Cassidy and the Sundance Kid covered the back wall.

The food was wonderful. We learned that Jay's boss, the restaurant owner, traveled regularly to Central America to see family, so she knew the culture and cuisine quite well. And we were thankful. As much as we enjoyed the food of our travels, it was a nice reprieve to eat something that, in a roundabout way, reminded us of home.

We had our fill and stayed a little longer to enjoy the friendly atmosphere. It was nighttime when we reemerged onto the streets, and a number of pubs were open for business. They were bursting at the seams, actually. Wales had made it to the EuroCup quarter finals that weekend, and citizens filled the streets to show their support. Teenagers and young adults stumbled out of one pub and into the next, singing together and chanting their country's name like a war cry. The celebration rang on, and we walked through casually, enjoying their gladness.

At one point we passed a chanting gang and Tom joined in.

"Wales! Wales! Wales! Wales!"

We continued walking, but the gang stopped chanting and called after us.

"Hey, where're you guys from," one asked us.

"The United States," Philip answered, and tension hung in the air between us.

They didn't want to fight, did they? It was hard for us to tell in their drunken stupor, but it seemed as if they were processing what Philip had said. We stood at odds, our gang and theirs. Then the one who asked the question took a deep breath and—

"Wales! Wales! Wales," he began chanting again, and his crew rejoined him.

They turned back to the pubs, chanting, and we went our own way. Whatever they thought of us, they had moved on.

We reached our bed-and-breakfast a few blocks later but decided to continue down to the pier. The ferry port was off to our right, but this area held a hundred sailboats, anchored for a quarter mile out on the bay. Our team gathered on the pier, going out as far as possible. At the edge, we stood in the dark, looking over the black water. Streaks of light danced on the ripples, reflecting stars and the moon overhead. It was so quiet and simple.

"You should give a speech," Luke said to me, and the others agreed.

I thought for a moment, recalling our trip thus far. We had seen cities and open fields, flown over an ocean and walked by a river, and to me it was all breathtaking. And this place was no different. I recalled a hymn of old.

"They told us not to come here," I said. "They said Holyhead was a lousy place. But I say, this is my Father's world, and it is beautiful."

We slept well that night in Holyhead and boarded our ferry the next morning.

PHILIP'S POINT OF VIEW

Hearing Kevan describe the experience of walking in the woods carried me to a renewed appreciation and wonder for things that are, for me, everyday occurrences. Walking in the woods, standing at people's eye level, going up and down stairs, running, dancing. I heard Kevan remark about these on our trip, and I realized how little gratitude I have for the "ordinary."

Kevan is an example of appreciation and gratitude for life, and throughout our trip and my friendship with him, I saw that infectious spark travel to those he came in contact with.

14

TURBULENCE

WHILE WE WERE ABLE TO TRAVEL through France and England using well-connected public transit systems (buses, trains, subways), our journey across Ireland would be more direct by renting a van. So we came into Dublin on a ferry and took two buses to the airport, and there we made arrangements to rent a passenger van to drive from one end of the country to the other.

As we'd done a dozen times on trains, we set me on the bench seat—still in the backpack. I sat in the middle and, for safety, we had a guy on each side and a seat belt strapped over the front of the pack, just under my knees. My feet, in their hip stirrups, were propped on the bench beneath me. And as we piled into the van for the four-hour drive across Ireland, all felt secure. We were going on fifteen days with no serious injury, and we were feeling a tinge of invincibility.

Our drive was a mix of highways and country roads. We passed hamlets and castles as you would gas stations in Kansas. There was a relaxed spirit among the team. Half the van was asleep, the other half sat quietly, contentedly, watching the green world roll by—until we hit the brakes at sixty-five miles per hour.

Toll roads in Ireland are different from toll roads in the States. I wish I understood what exactly happened, but it went something like this: A toll barricade dropped down in front of us at the most inconvenient moment, and to avoid hitting it, our driver slammed on the brakes. This tested the integrity of my setup.

With the force of our sudden stop, my top-heavy backpack tipped forward. Seat belts are designed for such a time, but not for such a backpack. The belt gave way, and in the blink of an eye my face was planted into the seat in front of me. It only took a split second, but everyone in the van snapped wide awake, and they all gathered to right my fall. I took inventory of my body, noting a great throb in my left foot (over the toes particularly) and an aching throughout my head. I had hit it pretty hard.

"Kevan," Philip asked, "you okay?"

"Oh," added Ben, pointing to my face. "I don't think so."

I felt warm liquid roll out of both nostrils, and there was a gash at the bridge of my nose. Robbie, our medical expert, jumped into action and staunched the bleeding with rags.

Next thing I knew, we were in a gas station parking lot. The guys had me sitting on the ground beside our van. They were icing my foot and taping up my nose. They asked me to move my toes, to make sure they weren't broken, and I followed someone's finger with my eyes too. Ben got bottled waters from inside, and then they all huddled around me while I tried to calm down.

Two thoughts held my mind captive. The first: *This foot will scream with pain for the rest of our trip. Nothing will be comfortable.* With weak muscles and a habit of not looking where I was going, I grew up with sprained feet and twisted ankles. I knew this feeling, and I knew what it would feel like for the next few weeks. The second thought: *Sure, I've bloodied my nose before, but I've never outright broken it. Will it heal crooked?* Chandlers take pride in their straight, regal noses. It's one of the things my mom boasts about in her boys. This sent me spiraling into a ridiculous identity crisis, founded in my state of shock. I spent the rest of the day studying my nose, cross-eyed, to see how off-centered it might be.

I felt warm liquid roll out of both nostrils, and there was a gash at the bridge of my nose.

As I sat on the asphalt in that parking lot, I remember being overwhelmed by the situation. The pain that raced through me was a wicked bully pressing my face into the dirt, telling me I had tried and failed, and it was time to give up the fight. Maybe it was time to just go home.

Today's culture cushions the disabled, sheltering us and trying to make us as comfortable as possible. We're feeble, helpless, pitiful. But I'd pushed back against that idea—I have my whole life— making the argument that a full life supersedes comfort, and I'm stronger than I look. I can handle as much hardship as the next guy, regardless of my disability. Just because I'm in a wheelchair doesn't mean I have to be spoon-fed and surrounded by pillows. It was a point of conversation as we designed the backpack. What's a little discomfort when you're having such a great adventure? I wanted to show the world that taking some risks was okay, and maybe even not a big deal. Just go out and try, get out of your comfort zone and live. But I hadn't considered that there's a big difference between discomfort and pain, between risk and actual injury.

The able-bodied world, I thought, watched me like watching a duck cross the road, hoping he'd make it across, the underdog spirit cheering for me to succeed. The disabled community looked on with bated breath, like I was Evel Knievel, hoping I'd break the mold for us all. What started as a few friends going on a trip had turned at some point into a mission, in my heart at least, to change the world. And the duck just got hit by a car. Evel Knievel just wrecked his bike. I had broken my nose. I had come frighteningly close to breaking my foot. I more than likely had a concussion. And I was 3,500 miles from home. My head filled with a barrage of voices—teachers, doctors, parents of other disabled kids: "This is why," they said, pointing fingers at my swollen face. "This is why we shelter you. This is what happens if you go out there like you're invincible. You just can't do things like the other boys. When we said it was too dangerous, this is what we meant. Now look at you."

I had tried, arrogantly, to prove a point, and in the moment, it seemed to me like it had all backfired in the blink of an eye. Who did I think I was, getting caught up in the hype of my own foolishness? I lived in a dream world. I had convinced people this was a good idea, that I could push the limits, and once I'd convinced enough people, I began to believe it myself. But who am I, really? I'm just a crippled kid with some lucky breaks, and that luck just ran out on an Irish highway. The sky isn't the limit. Some things really aren't possible. Some things should be left to the imagination.

Who did I think I was, getting caught up in the hype
of my own foolishness? . . . I'm just a crippled kid
with some lucky breaks, and that luck just ran out.

I knew this position well. I knew this feeling of defeat as surely as I felt the pain in my foot. I'd felt it before in life, in low moments—emergency room visits, the loss of loved ones, shortcomings, rejections—those times in life when you feel like it's all catching up to you and it's more than you can bear. Those times, in truth, when we are weakest.

I did the only thing I knew to do—I pressed into the Lord. I didn't need to fill him in on the details; he saw it all for himself. And I wasn't in much of a state to articulate it anyway. I was scared, hurt, and I felt alone against a watching world that had tried to warn me for the past thirty years. I needed a fighter in my corner, whether I was right or wrong. In this moment, at my weakest, I needed someone bigger than me to take over for a while, so I asked God for that, and this is what happened: I realized I was surrounded already—I had six fighters in my corner. They had carried me this far, and what I saw clearly was that they weren't finished yet. They were here for me on my good days as well as my worst.

Tom squatted to my right, Robbie to my left, Ben behind me, Philip in front, and Luke and Mr. Hill behind Robbie. I found strength in these men, a peace about them that guarded my heart and mind. I asked Tom to put his arm around me, which he did, and this loosed my dammed-up tears. I wept at the pain, at the anxious lies running through my head, and at the amazing love of God and my brothers here that held me up.

After about an hour, we decided to continue our drive. Portmagee awaited us. Our journey wasn't over. We went on into the night, reflective for a while, and then slowly found our goofy courage again. Throughout the rest of the drive, whether the van was filled with silence or laughter, a smell lingered with me: the smell of dried blood in my nose. It reminded me, with every breath, of the challenges I face and the victories I find, not in my own strength or courage, but in those who love me—my family, my friends, and my God.

TOM'S POINT OF VIEW

One of us lost his driving privileges for the remainder of the trip. It's just as well. Who let me, the guy who doesn't even own a car—who spent the past five years commuting to work by bike—get behind the wheel in a foreign country?

I'm just glad my wife wasn't driving. She still has an outstanding speeding ticket in Spain. I'll never forget the sound of her maniacal laughter in that mountain range after we dodged the oncoming traffic while passing a truck at 140 million kilometers per hour, her beautiful blond hair blowing in the arid Iberian wind. Love, indeed. Love gets us into all kinds of trouble.

15

SKELLIG MICHAEL

IN THE SUMMER OF 2015, I was hospitalized. I was there overnight, and Ben (ever faithful) slept on the couch by my bed to keep me company. Before turning off the light, he pulled out his Bible and began flipping through it. We were both exhausted. The hour was lost on us; it had been a long day. I was almost zonked out, but I managed a sigh and spoke.

"What's up?"

"I just thought I'd read a little before bed," he said with a yawn.

"Do you mind reading aloud?" I asked.

"Sure, man, if you want me to. Have anything in mind?"

"No," I said, half asleep already. "I'm up for whatever."

Ben flipped through the thin pages for another minute and then settled somewhere in the middle.

"A psalm?" I guessed.

"Yeah," he said, getting comfortable in his makeshift bed. "Psalm twenty-nine. It might be one of my favorites."

And so we fell asleep in a hospital room to the song of David, and a year later, those words would return to me on a cliff in Ireland.

* * *

We arrived at Portmagee the night of July 3, greeted by the final chords of a jam session in our hotel's pub. The town is a cozy fishermen's strip of inns and shops right off the pier. We were told the time of breakfast (quite early, compared to our last two weeks), "and then you just cross the street to the boats."

That was our plan for Monday, the Fourth of July. While our friends and family back home partook of hotdogs and fireworks, we would take a boat to Skellig Michael and climb six hundred steps to the top. We had trained, physically and emotionally, for months, developing techniques and building team unity. The day would be ours.

Robbie's alarm went off, echoed shortly by Ben's. The sun woke around the same time, and Tom came in from his room to give me a bath. I remember dozing in the tub, and next thing I knew I found myself in the pack and we were on our way through the corridors down to the pub.

My face and foot still ached from the accident, but it seemed fitting for the adventure we were setting out to have. It is a strange phenomenon, with guys in particular, that pain somehow enhances the depth of our doing. *Die Hard, Gladiator, Taken*—broken nose or a mortal wound can do wonders for a man's confidence. I could've done without my foot pulsating at every step, but my disdain for the pain only made my resolve greater. It reminded me that life has its moments of pain, and you need to roll with them and keep going or you'll never accomplish much of anything. If this had been a completely incident-free trip, I think we would've felt cheated somehow. So we walked the corridors down to the pub. We were groggy and sore and broken—and ready to take on the world.

It is a strange phenomenon, with guys in particular,
that pain somehow enhances the depth of our doing.

A word about those corridors. I never made sense of them in the three days we were there. Perhaps M. C. Escher was involved in the design or was an inspiration at least. The staircases were short and frequent, the next never going the same direction as the last and ending often at blind corners. In connection to these puzzle-piece rises, hallways long and short boasted low ceilings and antiquated artwork of oceans and boats, bait and tackle. Some of the hallways had doors to rooms, and some were like secret passages from one staircase to another. Mind you, major factors in my discombobulation might have been my tiredness and the unfamiliar height at which I experienced such spaces. After thirty years of life at a four-foot perspective, the world at a sudden six foot five is a difficult thing to process. My spatial wherewithal was often thrown off, as was my concept of time. So I wasn't surprised when others navigated the mazes just fine. I, however, was completely lost, and I was anxious for the wide-open spaces of the sea and the island that awaited us.

Our breakfast was the traditional Irish sort, similar to our English experience. Due to our limited time, I opted for pancakes, which proved (to my delight) to be more like crepes. I gobbled down the nearly translucent sweets and chased them with a cup of hot tea. In the time it took me to eat this, the guys downed mountains of eggs and sausage and assorted fruits. Of course they did.

As we finished up our meal, the innkeeper came to our table. She was a sun-worn woman in her late-fifties, broad-shouldered and motherly. It was this woman who bore us the unfortunate news. The elements were not favorable. Winds were too high and waters too choppy. The boats wouldn't be going out, and we'd just have to try for tomorrow. Our heads sank with discouragement. We'd faced all the odds so far, gone up against train schedules, foreign languages, weird old ladies, wrong directions, museum security, poor planning, allergies, injuries, fatigue, and drunk people. We had pulled off the impossible, or at least the crazy, and landed on our feet. But the weather is something else entirely, one of God's great equalizers, and we only had one more chance before our time there was up. Some of the team cleared out to clean up or use the restroom or grab seconds. I remained at the table, considering the day. My heart, I realized, was actually pretty light on the matter, though I couldn't decide why.

"You all right, man?" Luke asked, sitting next to me.

There's a sincerity in Luke that I admire. "Yeah," I answered honestly. "Tomorrow will be fine. It'll happen."

"Oh yeah," he agreed with certainty.

* * *

We decided that though it was too drafty to go out to sea, we could take to the land well enough. We'd brought a set of trekking poles with us, specifically for stability on the island, and this was a good time to test them out. Near the inn, just to the right of the pier, stretched a bridge across the inlet to a wide green hill. A pebble- and scrub-colored beach spread at the knoll's foot.

Robbie opted for a nap back in our room (who could blame him). The others bundled up and took me traipsing over to the beach. The wind was sharp on our ears and even challenged our balance as we crossed the bridge.

"Can we move away from the edge?" I asked as we walked along curbs.

They had it under control, of course. These guys had been walking on curbs and bridges for twenty-some years, but they obliged my requests with abounding grace. Well, most of the time. There are times in life when we need to be pushed beyond our limits, and the guys embraced those occasions with audible joy. Especially Tom.

Tom carried me as we reached the end of the bridge. We turned left, cut through a field, and stepped onto a dock. It stretched over the scrub beach to touch the water's edge. The beach rested far below, undisturbed, and a chain barrier lined the dock to keep us hemmed in. Beyond the chain, a stack of slate sheets acted as the dock's base and—Tom decided—our stairway to the beach.

"This looks like a good spot," he said, taking hold of the chain.

"Good for what?" I asked, trying to hide my nerves.

Last time he said that, he left me alone in a field, which was awesome. But I had a feeling that wasn't his plan this time. Tom has a wide smile, the kind you can see from the back of his head. And I saw it then as he studied the sheer rock layers at his toes. The wind cut through us like a knife through ripe pears.

"Well," he said matter-of-factly. "These look comparable to the steps on Skellig."

"Yeah," I added, "but there's a chain keeping us off of them."

"Oh, we can climb over that," he said, proving it with a long-legged straddle of the chain.

Were we breaking the law? There was no one watching, no one around to tell us whether we were or not. Maybe the chain was just there for our safety, to prevent us from trying to, you know, climb the rocks—like we were doing.

Philip held the trekking poles while Tom and I, now on the dangerous side of the chain, steadied ourselves on the first slab. Tom reached back, so casually, to retrieve the poles. I looked down, and two things registered with me—the beach below and the way down to it, or rather, the lack of a way down to it. Where would Tom step? This was a moment, like so many others, when I needed to trust my friends and their able legs. Tom giggled at the adventure, planting his poles on the lower slate.

"Okay, we're going to go here," he said, stepping down and to the right. "And here," to the left. "And here."

Before I knew it, we were on level ground. We'd arrived at the beach, and the countless pebbles moved like awakened beetles under our weight. Tom held his balance with steady knees and firmly set poles. We walked carefully toward the ocean, every step rolling and grinding the smooth stones together. Moss and weeds clung to the wet earth against an unbearable wind. The foliage cumulated in mounds so that sometimes Tom found himself ankle-deep in the soggy stuff.

We strode through the marshy world, like stranded explorers on a deserted planet. Philip and Ben lingered nearby, taking in the strange land with caution and intrigue. Our film crew collected data, recording samples and tracking weather patterns. Tom trudged on, while I kept a wary eye peeled for alien beasts who might emerge from the moss piles or even the listless tide.

We ventured under the dock and to the other side of the beach, where we found boulders to climb. And climb we did, all four of us, and we stood high, swaying in the wind like reeds. Ben had a coffee with him, befitting his casual nature, and Philip was inquisitive of the fauna, befitting his. Tom and I turned circles on the rock, scanning the horizon like shepherds, then climbed down. It was time to ascend again, back to civilization.

"So," I said, "we're going back around, right? Back up the way we came?"

"No," Tom replied, heading straight for another section of the wall. "This part will do just fine."

Of course. We can't return to the familiar, I thought. *What would be the fun in that?*

Luke appeared overhead, spry Inigo awaiting Westley's arrival. Philip and Ben stayed close behind us in case of a misstep, and Tom struck the rock with his trekking poles. One step, two step, a stretch to number three, then a few short steps like stairs to a stoop and we were there. Safely back up top, we wandered a bit more and eventually headed back to our rooms at the hotel, where we crashed for a few hours.

* * *

When I awoke, Ben and Robbie were gone. They had set out on foot to see the legendary Cliffs of Kerry, so the rest of us hopped into our van and headed that way. We met them on the road and collected them. By this time, they'd already visited the cliffs and were on their way farther down the narrow road to a chocolate factory. They were kind enough to rejoin us on the cliffs, and we enjoyed a walk along the edge of the world.

A gaunt creature greeted us at the gate, exchanging coins for admittance. His curious face caught my eye, and I let my mind wander into an imagined story of his life. His name is Thom Don Diggle, and he's never left County Kerry. Our innkeeper is his mum, and his pop was killed by a squall when he was nine years old. Thom wears his father's sweater now, and he took this ticket job at the cliffs to keep from being recruited by the fishermen below. Every night, when the gate closes and it's just him and the cliffs, he scales to the highest point and regales his ghost-father with the events of the day. He makes up stories about the people he's seen and the ghosts they probably talk to at night, because he assumes that's just what everyone does. Also, he's an expert at the yo-yo. I'm at least half-convinced that's all true. You would be too if you saw him.

We can't return to the familiar, *I thought.*
What would be the fun in that?

The path up to the cliffs was long and smooth, but as soon as we crested to see the ocean, my attention was captured by our surroundings. Green fields to my right and left bowed under the wind's terrible weight. I, too, bowed as the air pressed into my whole existence like a wraith with broad black wings. The closer we came to the cliffs, the more violent the winds grew, and my friends hunched their shoulders for shelter. It was a presence, this living, breathing pressure upon us, and it tore at the world mercilessly. We pushed forward, up and up around the Ring of Kerry, until we reached a place of observation, and then we moved closer to the edge, gripping the cold railing with white knuckles.

Ben steadied the backpack from behind as Tom and I leaned out over the railing and looked down. Oh, how the waters raged! As I watched the mighty waves thrash like dragons and as I felt the winds beating me into submission, I knew full well the terrible power of creation. I was being crushed and suffocated, overwhelmed by its enormity. The deafening roar of a thousand ancient lions laid claim to my bones and soul. Then, amid the din, a hymn filtered through, the Holy Spirit singing the song of David.

"The voice of the Lord is over the waters. The God of glory thunders over many waters." And then, "The voice of the Lord makes the deer give birth and strips the forests bare."

Psalm 29 tells of power, not the power evident in the splendor of nature but in the Lord's eminent reign over it all. Suddenly the wild world on whose edge I stood played a beautiful role in revealing Christ. The perspective was clear and unbreaking. As though faced with a furious bear that's held at bay by a masterful rider, I quake at the former, but that quaking is nothing compared to my awe of the latter. So the earth. So all of creation. That it's Keeper should oversee, nod, and deny, give life and destroy it—what a King! What a Lord!

In the song David declares, "All in his temple cry, 'Glory!'" and I found myself with the same word on my lips. Terror and comfort folded into one new sensation as a smile crept over my face. The wind continued its surge, the waves carried on their tantrum, and I began to laugh. I let that crazy wind fill my lungs. I loosed my gaze on the ocean and saw its truth. God's great hands press into these elements, hold them in place, and churn them to his will. And all in his temple cry, "Glory!"

"Thank you, Lord," I whispered, and he heard me through the cacophony.

Farther up the ring we climbed, farther along the cliff's edge, until we arrived at the highest point. It was a thin peninsula that jutted out into the ocean like a knife. And out on the tip of that knife I went with my friends. And there we met a revelatory view. Through the gray haze, some seven miles off, we saw her, bold and brooding.

Skellig Michael.

It has a masculine name, but we'd taken to calling it a woman. And now we stood, looking her in the eye. We'd talked about her, considered her, studied her, but now she was right there. The team collected around me, like a gang preparing to fight. I stared her down and she stared right back, just as hard, just as conscious, and just as ready for tomorrow.

The deafening roar of a thousand ancient lions
laid claim to my bones and soul.
Then, amid the din, a hymn filtered through,
the Holy Spirit singing the song of David.

"Dude," Ben said at my left shoulder. "You got this."

This would not be the last time he'd need to remind me.

A swelling came to my chest, a crinkle in my eye, a smirk at the corner of my lip.

In the psalm, David goes on about the power of God Almighty. Creative, destructive, sovereign, all-consuming. "The Lord sits enthroned over the flood; the Lord sits enthroned as king forever." And then he ends with this: "May the Lord give strength to his people! May the Lord bless his people with peace!" This settled into me as I stood with my friends, staring down the legend, that unreachable, untouchable lady of the Irish coast. She was there. We'd flown over waters, taken trains, ridden ferries; I'd broken my nose on my way to her; and now we were here, standing so close, we could see her—closer, already, than anyone ever dreamed I could be.

But this wasn't it, just standing here, staring. No. Tomorrow. Tomorrow, I'd take her on.

God's charge to man in Genesis took on new meaning then, that "man should have dominion of the earth." Not only should we tend to it and protect it, but we have freedom over it too. Because of the Lord's promise, explorers can look upon the white world of Antarctica and say, "I will know you." The merchants of another age could look out toward the unmapped blues and say, "We will go." And I can look at Skellig Michael and say, "I will climb you." The world is ours to care for and ours to enjoy from start to finish, top to bottom, and all its wonders in between.

"Tomorrow," I said low to the island before me. "Tomorrow, you're mine."

And she whispered back, "Bring it on."

* * *

That night, weary from the day, I took to my room. Ben sat on the bed with his phone while I sat sideways in the backpack nearby. I was journaling about the day while awaiting a video call from my sister. Throughout the trip, we'd kept up by email and brief video chats. Same with my parents, and I figured it was time I told them about the accident. Its effect would, after all, start showing up in pictures online, and they'd want to hear it from me first. I dreaded the call, though. What should I fear more, the wrath of my sister or my mom? I was in a sort of stupor, waiting.

Finally, the call came and I answered.

My sister, Connie, is lovely and wonderful. She is my most kindred of spirits and the closest of friends. But she *is* my older sister, and she inhabits the role well by pestering me with concern and correction.

I can look at Skellig Michael and say,
"I will climb you." The world is ours to care for
and ours to enjoy from start to finish,
top to bottom, and all its wonders in between.

When I answered her video call, I did so with my nose out of frame.

"I need to tell you something," I confessed pretty quickly.

"Okay," she answered slowly. "What happened?"

I prefaced that I was okay, then I explained the accident.

"So I messed up my foot a bit," I said, "and I broke my nose."

I moved my full face into view, and what followed was no small commotion.

"Oh, honey!" was all she could say.

Then Mom and Dad had to be told.

My father is a temperate man. He came in and rested an elbow on the back of Connie's chair, studying the screen from afar. Then

Mom entered, laundry in her arms, and leaned into the screen.

"Hey, Kev!" she said, glad to see me.

Connie beat me to the punch. "He broke his nose."

"What?! What happened?"

I explained as briefly as possible and then braced for impact. Mom stood there for a second, processing the news. Then she furrowed her brow.

"But you're okay otherwise?" she asked.

"Yeah, I'm fine."

"Okay," she said. "When will you be home? I'll have the boys here and they'll be in your room."

Ben looked up from his bed across the room, surprise claiming us both. I'd forgotten that my brother's kids were visiting. The conversation moved on to everything *but* my injuries, and then it was time to say goodbye. I hung up with a sigh of relief. *That was too easy*, I thought. She had her hands full, getting ready for their arrival, and she didn't have time to worry about me. Being the youngest, I would typically be jealous of the attention my mom gave to my nephews, but this time it actually came in handy.

* * *

As night fell on us that July 4, the team gathered to discuss the potentials of the following day. Not only had we been told the current weather was no good for the boats, but we found out this had been the case for the past four days. And this meant three things: the likelihood of another bad day for weather was high, the line of waiting customers was piling up, and more people meant less room for all of us to go together. Fair? Unfair? It's just the real world. So we seven foreigners sat down around my bed and made the hard decisions.

Our best possible situation would be a clear day (dreary and cold, but calm on the water). We would all get onto the island by one boat, have a grand ol' hiking time, and return to a welcoming party and ice cream bar. This was our wildest dream, but options had to be weighed and possibilities considered.

If the elements said no again, we'd have to head home. We simply couldn't wait around another day on the off chance that the weather would clear. This was a point of lengthy conversation, but some things are just out of your control. Funds were waning and so was our energy. We were at our end on all fronts, so it was sadly decided that July 5 was the last call and we'd hope for the best.

If the elements said no again, we'd have to head home. . . .
Funds were waning and so was our energy.

And what if we couldn't all go? The question had to be asked. I was torn on the matter. This was my team. We were a unit and part of one another by now. We were Spartans, and Skellig was our Thermopylae. Everyone played a role, and every role was essential. But this was why we came, the pinnacle of our journey, so we determined to go, even if some had to stay behind.

Robbie was the first to speak up.

"I'm good with not going," he said. "I came into the team later anyway."

"Yeah," Ben added. "I think the original four should take priority."

He was speaking of Tom, Philip, Luke, and myself. He pointed out that we'd been working to get here for over a year, and Mr. Hill agreed. The four of us were humbled. We felt the weight of the decision—but it was made. Our hope was for the whole group to go, but (weather and God permitting) at least the four of us would be on a boat. With that, we called it a night and headed to bed.

Ben and Robbie stayed with me again, to ensure Tom and Philip were rested up for the hike. Tom and Philip didn't rest well, though. They paced their room half the night, fretting about the climb. Tom was especially concerned about the step from dry boat to wet rock. To be honest, I don't remember how I slept or if I dreamed. I don't remember going to bed or getting up early again. Did breakfast happen that morning? I'd already gone through that epic procession the day before—suiting up, mentally preparing, the maze-walk to breakfast, and so on. The formalities had passed and now there was nothing left but to get on the boat.

Thus, my memory of the day begins on the pier.

LUKE'S POINT OF VIEW

The possibility of missing Skellig Michael didn't exist. Not in my mind, at least. This was the last leg of the trip, and I knew that our purpose and our story had already been set in motion. Anything that happened now was a new branch on a seed planted back in the Paris Metro.

I approach all new challenges from a similar perspective: everything is easier the second time. When I played baseball as a teenager, a coach gave me a piece of advice that I still think about often: "Imagine yourself stepping up to the plate and making contact with the ball. Then do it." I'm not talking about manifest destiny or projected reality. I fail often. For me, visualizing a goal keeps my anxiety in check and helps me focus on what I already know how to do.

We had everything we needed to scale that mountain. Do variables exist? Always. Do planning and practice help? They're essential. But we had already climbed Skellig, if only in our imaginations, and we were ready to go again.

16

ASCENT

I was on Tom's back, bundled to the gills in a coat and beanie, and we stood with Philip amid a waiting crowd. A rounded man—we would soon learn his name was Pat Joe—came up from the bobbing fleet of boats and grumbled his way through the crowd. He was looking for us, as it turned out, and greeted us with a wipe of his mouth. Pat Joe had, I'm convinced, no eyes. And below the empty black slits where they should have been hung scruffy cheeks around a handful of teeth. His skin, like our innkeeper's, was sun-dried and swollen from an epoch of squinting. As he spoke to us, it was like he was talking to himself and we just happened to be there to hear it. His words seemed to snuggle deep into those pillowy jowls and fall asleep before they could reach us, but he would cough and sputter them awake and they'd stumble out drowsily.

Pat Joe explained to us that, due to the buildup of customers because of the recent weather, he couldn't guarantee all of us going. He wanted to try, though, and thought maybe we could come in on separate boats, four of us on one and three on another. He asked if that was all right with us and we said sure.

We liked him.

His mannerisms betrayed annoyance, but I got the impression it wasn't us who bothered him. At least, not our group in particular. Maybe he just missed having the port, water, and island all to himself and his friends. Within the past few months, the place had been flooded with pop culture fans and screaming, spoiled kids. It used to be a quiet town, tucked away from the madness of Hollywood and Facebook. But now Americans came in droves on their religious pilgrimages to see where Luke Skywalker stood at the end of *Star Wars: The Force Awakens*, bringing with them cameras, iPhones, and lightsabers. I wonder how early he got up that morning just to enjoy the peace and stillness of God's creation before business kicked in for the day.

He led the four of us to his boat and the rest of our team to another one nearby. They would wait there in case openings came available, and it was looking good for them. Our boat began to fill up as Pat Joe checked his riggings and motor. His elbows bent to rest his arms over his belly, his tree-stump hands poking out of his forest-green sweater. He never stopped moving, looking this way and that, taking a new deep breath with every shuffled step, like he carried sandbags in his tattered, old shoes. I enjoyed watching him while we waited for the launch. He tickled my spirit and gave it courage—as ancient, hardworking men are wont to do to spirits.

The sun shone down on us through a clear blue sky, bringing warmth and light like a playful jab at yesterday's chilly gray. I couldn't help but laugh at the heavens' favor, and it added a kind of hope to the day. Philip applied sunscreen to us all while Luke checked over his gear one last time.

An older couple who spoke little English climbed into our boat, followed by a much younger couple and a family who were quintessentially American. All aboard were fine enough company, and it seemed to us that we'd launch any minute and meet the other guys there. But just as Pat Joe untied us from the dock, Ben appeared with a sad smirk and an outstretched hand.

"It's all you, guys," he said, and Tom took his hand. "The other boat filled up."

Americans came in droves on their religious pilgrimages to see where Luke Skywalker stood at the end of Star Wars: The Force Awakens, *bringing with them cameras, iPhones, and lightsabers.*

A panic rushed into me. It was always a possibility, of course. We knew this and had planned accordingly, but I had hoped and prepared for the challenge with our whole team in mind. The whole trip had been a wild ride of flying by the seat of our pants, and I'd rolled with all of it just fine, but this rocked me. My countenance drooped, but Ben countered it with a mischievous smile. He looked long and hard at each of us and gave a brotherly nod.

"Hey," he said with the confidence of a hero. "You got this."

Waving aside our friend like a seagull in his way, Pat Joe loafed himself into the little boat and cranked up the motor. Ben rejoined Robbie and Mr. Hill on the pier as we scooted off through the bay. Mr. Hill managed to slip onto a boat tour encircling Skellig Michael while the other two hiked into the hills and explored castle ruins. They split off toward these endeavors as we exited the bay slowly, its green mouth spilling us out into the wide sea ahead. Once the cliffs and hill country were behind us, and the waters proved their true boundless nature, Pat Joe throttled us into a deafening flight over the blue world.

The island and her lesser twin were at my back, out of sight. Our ride to them was a little less than an hour, loud, and taken at a steady clip. However, a funny thing happens when land is gone and the skies are clear. Save for the occasional puffin, there's no spatial frame of reference. And the droning of the motor for that long scrambles your sense of time and sound. Essentially, abandoned to such blank vastness, we succumb to a sort of numb transcendence. Time hung itself out to dry as my mind wandered through catalogues of nautical literature.

"No man is an island," John Donne wrote from his deathbed, "entire of itself."

But maybe he is. Maybe man is alone. After all, the preacher wrote this in exile, listening to death bells toll just outside his window. I juxtaposed his thought to that of Tom Hanks in *Joe Versus the*

Volcano. "There are doors you gotta go through alone, ya know?" Maybe man is more of an island than Donne wanted to admit as he faced down death and knew everyone else would face it, too, in their own exiles.

Morose, I know, hopeless. I shook off this train of thought and quieted my mind.

"Lord," I prayed, "you brought me here, and these thoughts are weary drivel, not of you. Please take captive my mind. I'm pressing into you. Reveal yourself to me."

Maybe man is more of an island than Donne
wanted to admit as he faced down death. . . .
I shook off this train of thought and quieted my mind.

Around this time the ten-year-old sitting beside Philip lost his breakfast to the rocking waves. His mother let out a cry and held him halfway over the boat's side. The father did a double take at his vomiting son and then focused his camera on the approaching Lesser Skellig.

We noticed Philip was not far from the same fate as the boy. He sat with his head between knees, eyes shut tight. It came as a surprise to all of us, including Philip, but he was nauseated, and had no escape. He set himself back on the bench and rubbed his belly, shaking his head in disbelief.

"Man," he said miserably, "I know how that kid feels."

Tom patted Philip on the shoulder.

"We'll be there soon," I said.

We looked up, then, to see Lesser Skellig creep into view beside us. She was like a stone fortress rising high overhead, jagged and menacing. Long, dark rocks arced together like buttresses to form a world ruthless to man and heavenly to native fowl. The ocean blasted against her base like an army attempting siege, and the castle loomed, ancient and strong.

She wasn't a sage like her sister. Her age had not fostered wisdom but a sort of tired lunacy. I was reminded of G. K. Chesterton's line from his novel *The Napoleon of Notting Hill*: "I have survived the Deluge. I am a pyramid, and must behave as such." How apropos, and how much more literal here than Chesterton ever intended. A white film shrouded the shoulders of the rocks as gulls perched and shifted, hopped and soared around their sanctum. She stood still as a grandmother, a refuge for her birds from the miles of swallowing blue and treacherous gales. And our tug sputtered on by, adding mere ripples to the rage at her feet.

I watched her go, wondering at her haunted shelter until we were back out on the open water. Skellig Michael loomed just up ahead, but she was still out of sight at my back. For all I knew, we could be one mile away or another five. Time was suspended again as space gave way to waves, the hum of the engine, and sunlight. Suddenly Pat Joe cut the motor, and we coasted gently over the rolling water.

We must be close, I thought.

And then I felt her.

Skellig Michael is not an island. She is a world, with moons and gravity and a beating heart at her core. She is a queen to be feared, respected, and loved all in the same breath. She is a presence, and her visitors know the power in her shadow.

Her shadow stretched over our boat. A weight came down on my shoulders like a blanket, the hand of God resting wide, calloused, and heavy, just behind my neck. I took in a long, deep breath. Tom did the same, his chest and shoulders expanding, collapsing, expanding again, and I fell into rhythm with him.

Skellig Michael is not an island.
She is a world, with moons and gravity
and a beating heart at her core.
She is a queen to be feared, respected,
and loved all in the same breath.

His slow breathing turned into a chuckle as our boat crawled up alongside the landing. Pat Joe looped a thick cord around a metal hook in the rock and held it taut to keep us close to the steps. Yes, the steps. These were Tom's greatest concern, and now we sat three feet from them.

Pat Joe motioned for us to go, but we let everyone else get off first. We decided it would be best to watch a few others, to learn from their efforts. The boat dipped and rose on a moody tide so that our guide had to instruct each passenger accordingly. He'd say to one, "Take the second step . . . now," and then to the next, "The first step . . . now."

A chain-link railing ran up the wall to safety, and when it was finally our turn, Tom clung to it with both hands. His grip was on the chain, his feet still on the boat. Tom is a mighty tall man, and for all the doorways I'd hit my head against while on his back, I was grateful now for his height—his ability to step far and reach even farther. We awaited Pat Joe's signal. The hull went up, down, up, down. We waited. The seaman studied the pattern, timed it with his black-slitted eyes. Then, "Second step," and . . . "now."

Tom launched himself upward. Hand over hand, foot over foot, we ascended at a steady pace.

I mimicked Ben's mantra: "You got this." And then my own: "You're doing great!"

Far above, everyone (those from our boat and others) leaned over the ledge to watch. They had all gone this route before us and knew the difficulty. And now they saw Tom do the same with me on his back. We reached the top, feeling the pride of Fezzik, and folks applauded, though there was an anxiety in all of us for what was to come.

* * *

From the landing, one takes a winding but level path around to the start of the climb. We took it easy, giving Philip time to settle his gut and collect himself. The walk involved a lot of pauses to look up at the towering country before us and to look down on the endless ocean from which we'd emerged. We had decided long ago that for the sake of safety, health, and pleasure, we would not rush ourselves. So this was a proper beginning, and we enjoyed our leisurely stroll to the starting line.

We turned a corner to find the stairs awaiting us. They were slabs of weathered rock, varied in size and shape, some loose, some unmoving. Standing there, leaning casually on a denim hip, was Bob, keeper of the Skellig grounds. Bob had a Willy Wonka kind of softness to his voice as he explained the rules of climbing. His long, gray hair fell back and poked out in tufts under his ears. He wore sunglasses and a slight smile that suggested approachability. There were a few points in his talk at which he turned his attention to our team specifically, encouraging a slow pace, careful spotting, and so on. Then, as his discourse ended, we were released, with more than thirty others, to proceed up the island.

But this is not an island in the traditional sense. There are no sandy shores to ease into, no trees to protect one from the elements. There are birds aplenty, but not nesting in the open, only tucked away and popping out when one least expects it. Skellig Michael is the peak of a mountain jutting out of the ocean. Most islands are this in some regard, their bases found on the ocean floor and rising to crest from the waves. But Skellig Michael is like the wicked cap of Mount Everest. She and her crazy sister are like crown tips of the Himalayas. When God formed the Rockies, he looked to the Skelligs (his work of earlier that day) for reference. Our path for the next two hours would be on gray stone with patches of green grace, all of it crooked, steep, worn, sacred. She is an arrowhead pointed heavenward, for saints and sinners alike to climb on trembling knees.

As we did when leaving the boat, we let most of the gaggle go before us. Bob drew near and gave us some pointers on places to look out for. He assured us we would be fine, after learning of our practices, and said he'd check in with us along the way too, just in case.

Our path for the next two hours would be
on gray stone with patches of green grace,
all of it crooked, steep, worn, sacred.

The first few steps were wide and deep, as easy as stepping onto a deck, and these carried us maybe ten to fifteen meters. Then a 180-degree turn to the right brought us to a narrow ledge that stretched over to the next set of steps. Philip went before us, Luke behind. Another short run of steps and then 90 degrees to the left. With each step, whether it was clearly stable or at all questionable, Tom took stock and planted his walking sticks well before moving.

* * *

I had hoped, along the way, that I'd find Jesus on this rock, that it would be a time of reflection and revelation, a profound awakening to internalize as we climbed. These are the expectations of a legless man, one who's never wrestled with stairs or known the focus of a strenuous hike. Even for me on my friends' backs, this part of the journey would take all my attention. I found myself as invested in the climb as Tom and Philip, embracing the stress of the body as we went. Great contributors to this were my recent injuries, primarily my foot, which hung in a stirrup at my carrier's hip. With every step, a throb of fire ran up through my left side. If nothing else brings you and keeps you in the present, pain will be ever faithful. I don't mean to say I was miserable—far from it! Just as pain draws one into reality, it enhances that reality and gives deeper value to the experience.

I had a friend once who took a walking tour overseas, and anytime his mind wandered, he stomped his foot to refocus himself. In the same way, the world opened up around me now as I saw it simply and fully in the ache of our physical efforts. *All body for now,* I told myself as we made our ascent. The spirit would sort itself out later. Little did I realize, the spirit works itself out, sometimes best, when it is left alone to its task, a tinker sequestered with his cogs and tools behind closed doors.

* * *

We came to a slight landing, grassy and flat, where folks slowed to rest. Here stood a rock weathered to resemble a hunched creature. They call it the Weeping Woman, and she stood in sad beauty against the unforgiving elements. In her I saw holiness surviving against darkness. The image pulled me through history, my own and more, to see the wickedness and harshness of a fallen creation and the righteousness of God, his grace and goodness, holding fast in the midst of it all. I saw war and suicide, hunger and hatred, and I saw Jesus pulling his cross uphill to make it all better. I saw hope itself standing against the whipping winds of a hopeless world and refusing to give way.

Turning from the woman, we looked up and Tom muttered, "This is it." Before us towered a rise of maybe 250 steps, straight up and narrow. These were the kind of stairs we'd come for, trained for, and so we rose. The higher we went, the farther the ocean seemed to stretch out around us. Folks had called this place other-worldly, and as we climbed I understood more and more why. Skellig is an alien planet of its own. Lost in time or transcendent of it, I'm not sure which, but it is out of touch and out of reach from the rest of the known world.

The sharp stone houses puffins. They nest deep in its crevices and pop out every once in a while to spy on what's happening on their porches. Tourists hike by like traffic on the highway, and I'm sure they curse us under their avian breath for waking their children at odd hours. And their yards do have some bits of green, though it's mostly scrubby weeds and lichen. It is lovely in a desolate, relic sort of way, like the moon or a fossil.

With each step Tom took, my head jostled lazily this way and that. When we first arrived on the island, we had untethered my neck pillow from the backpack, so that it was held only by my shoulders and neck. This allowed more freedom to adjust on the go, and allowed for more adjustment options as well, which were worth the looser fit it left us with. The trick here, as I've mentioned before, was to relax and not fight the movement. If I strained to hold my head still against the natural forces, I would have a steadier ride but grow tired sooner. So I let go and allowed myself to bobble for the sake of a long-term goal. No one said hiking would be easy or painless or give any sense of security. It's all quite the opposite, actually, but my, how fulfilling it is!

The image pulled me through history, my own and more,
to see the wickedness and harshness of a fallen creation
and the righteousness of God, his grace and goodness,
holding fast in the midst of it all.

Reaching the top of this rise brought us to an open plateau referred to as Christ's Saddle. To the right, another three hundred steps ran upward, and to the left, a ragged path led to a second peak. The former is the fifteen-hundred-year-old home of monks, and the latter is where, we learned, they fled to defend the island from pirates and Vikings. Before scaling either one, we stopped for a rest in the valley, sitting ourselves down in the soft grass. Others did the same. We brought a backpack (the normal kind) with supplies and food, and we rummaged inside it for sandwiches. PB&Js and water comprised our picnic on Christ's Saddle, overlooking an endless blue world before us. Once lunch was done, we stretched a bit, packed up, and got me onto Philip's back. He would carry me up to the monastery and back down to this spot before switching again with Tom for the descent. We opted for the climb to the monastery, as that was why we'd come all this way, and if we had time afterward, we'd check out the other peak.

Philip pressed upward, leaving behind the comfort of the Saddle. During this part of the ascension, we had a tall mountain wall on our right, like the steps were cut from the stone and room was hewn for the path. To our left, some partial rock formations tapered to a drop-off right into the cold, crashing water five hundred feet below. Drilled into the wall was a chain-link railing, like the one Tom had gripped to pull us off the boat earlier. Philip held this one just as firmly, Tom nearby for support and Luke capturing every step on film.

The steps here were taller, shallower, and steeper. Monks are no fools. If any unwanted visitors made it this far, their advances would stop (or at least slow) here, and a last line of holy defense could ward them off. There were no such monks awaiting us now, so we took our time going up safely.

A sharp right carried us farther up on a thin staircase until we reached a ledge like the one at the start, only much, much higher. From here, we could look out and down, seeing clearly where we'd come from and even our boat waiting patiently about a mile or so out. We paused in the open air to admire our achievement thus far, then proceeded along the ledge to meet a hefty stone doorway— our entrance to the monastery.

It was solid rock, and at least five feet through to the other side. The monks had defense in mind when they designed the passage, and so it was purposely difficult to navigate. The sturdy frame stood no more than four feet tall, a passage to be ducked through.

"We're gonna have to take you down," Tom said.

Philip squatted to see how low he could get, but ultimately he agreed. We all got into position for the dismount. Tom took hold of the backpack frame and Philip unbuckled himself. Typically at this point Philip would turn around right away and help Tom lower me to sit on the ground, but this was no time for rest. We had a lintel on a cliff's ledge to pass under, so he turned around and took hold, like always, and we moved in. They lowered me, but also themselves, and we three went through the ancient door together into a garden path trod once by holy men.

The steps here were taller, shallower, and steeper.
Monks are no fools. If any unwanted visitors made it this far,
their advances would stop (or at least slow) here,
and a last line of holy defense could ward them off.

It was a strip of dirt and gravel cutting through a sort of walled-in yard, and some folks stopped to take in the view. We paused long enough to remount me on Philip's back and continue on our way. The yard led to another short flight of stairs exposed entirely to the sky and ocean on our right. And these stairs rose to another door frame, very much like the last, so we repeated our tactic. It's nerve-tugging to climb open stairs on someone's back, but it's supremely nerve-*racking* to be taken on and off that back while on those open stairs. All it takes is one false move, and everything could spin out of control. This was another opportunity to exercise my trust in these dear men, and another opportunity for them to prove themselves equal to the task.

Coming up and out of the second doorway, we found ourselves finally in the heart of a monastery. And this is no conventional monastery, it must be said. I grew up reading *Redwall* books and hearing about St. Francis. Pictures were painted in my mind of castles and fortified villages with cattle and breweries and libraries within. Skellig Michael, though, bore on her ridgeback a cluster of crude stone huts, less than a dozen of them, and a chapel just as humble. The hut homes were built close to one another and stacked on various plateaus, to be reached by rough, tall, cramped sets of stairs.

The chapel looked just like the rest of the structures, save for its steeple and separation from the rest. Upon entering the cloister, the chapel stands straight ahead, at the edge of the world, and the hut barracks are ahead to the left. Behind the chapel is a small grave-yard, and between this and the constructs, there are thin aisles to reach each station.

Bordering the edge is a stone barrier maybe four feet high, and Philip took me there to take in the view. We leaned heavy on the wall, resting in the sunny morning, seven hundred feet above the ocean. We inhaled the fresh breeze; we surveyed God's vast creation. The clean skies framed a far-off mainland, green and lush, full of life. The men of Skellig, they say, came to the rock to commit their lives to Christ and prayer for their beloved Ireland. They looked upon it every day, and I wonder how their hearts sank, longing for home as they prayed earnestly for its redemption.

My heart ached for them, relating easily to their love for a fallen nation.

My foot ached as well. Philip felt me squirming to escape the pain, to try and find a comfortable position. Nothing. The pain persisted and I huffed at it. Philip felt that too.

A woman stood on one of the plateaus behind us, giving (in a lovely accent) commentary on the monastic life of old. She went into great detail about the monks' shelters and methods of gaining food (birds, fish, charity from the mainland). We overheard someone speak up in astonishment.

"These are terrible living conditions," he cried.

"Yes," she agreed amiably. "But the monks believed that every hardship is a prayer."

To this I had one response. It clicked into place in my heart and mind, and I began to laugh at the revelation. I patted Philip on the shoulder and laughed some more.

"Of course they did," I said to my friends. And then, "Okay."

I was now resigned. According to the Skellig monks, I'd said six hundred prayers coming up here and I was about to say six hundred more going down. Every hardship is a prayer, every spike of pain, every moment of discomfort. Every hardship is a prayer, an expression of our utter need for Christ and a calling out to him as "deep calls to deep." Paul says in his letter to the Romans, "We don't know how to pray, but the Holy Spirit intercedes for us with groanings too deep for words." Groanings may be a pain, may be an action, may be a sigh or a chuckle. Some things are too deep for words, and life is full of them. So we pray.

"Okay," I said, patting Philip on the shoulder, and we began our descent, a prayer in every step.

The throbbing pain continued. It grew worse. But I found my breath steady, my mind clear. We came to the first doorway and the guys lowered me, deciding to carry me between them to the next one. Once through the second doorway we were back on the ledge, looking down at the boats below. Pat Joe was there waiting for us. Tom lifted the pack and I was back onto Philip's shoulders, strapped in and ready to go.

Philip is a proactive man, and going down stairs is naturally a propelling motion, so we had to remind him repeatedly, "Watch your step, Philip. Take your time." I think it annoyed him a bit, but he understood and took heed with grace.

We came down off the ledge and followed the stairs back to Christ's Saddle, where we paused for another break. Tom pulled a surprise snack from his backpack—marzipan! My favorite treat! This was less about refueling, like lunch was, and more about celebration. We sat together on Christ's Saddle for the second time that day and took in the view. The first time we came as explorers, this time as conquerors.

Our marzipan ran out, and so did our time. We might have been conquerors, but if we didn't get moving, we would be stranded conquerors. So up I went onto Tom's back and down the stairs we continued. As fast as we wanted to go (for we knew Pat Joe was waiting), we also wanted to arrive safely, so we stepped carefully, and this caused a significant pileup of people behind us. It was embarrassing for us, and we stopped several times to let everyone pass. But each time the folks following us declined and cheered us on. They had been watching us the whole hike, braving what they braved, daring what they dared, and it encouraged them. I'd worried our shenanigans might mar their experience, but in fact we had enhanced it for them.

When we finally reached the bottom, we talked to the crowd and shared our story. Then it was off to find Pat Joe. Hopefully he hadn't left us. He'd threatened this, and we learned later from our fellow passengers that he'd considered it before we finally appeared. But there stood the grumbling man, holding taut the heavy rope, glaring at us with his black-slit eyes. We made our way down the stone steps onto the boat and thanked our skipper for waiting. He mumbled something that sounded half-approving, but it never quite made it out of his cheeks. We took our seats and he started up the motor.

Before leaving the island, Pat Joe took us for a circle around it. He showed us the old lighthouse, the new lighthouse, and a stairway older even than the ones we'd just climbed. It was the monks' earliest access point onto the island. The lighthouses were interesting enough, and though our backs were to them, we saw them as we rounded the island. But it was the ancient stairway that piqued something in us, and also in Pat Joe. The rest of our bench's company turned themselves to see the path, to ooh and ahh, but Tom and I, while curious, waited patiently. Maybe we'd catch a glimpse on our return. But Pat Joe came and stood beside us. We looked up at him, a rotund silhouette against the midday sun, his hair whipping in the sea's breezes.

"Woodja like I churn da boat aroond?" he asked.

"Huh?" Tom said, scrunching his nose.

I got it, and I tried to kindly decline.

"No," I said casually. "It's okay, really."

The silhouette waved me off, though, like a fly who didn't know what he wanted.

"I churn da boat aroond fur ya," he said dismissively.

Before we could object, Pat Joe was back at the helm and turning the boat so we could see clearly and unobstructed from our side. He took pride in this part of his tour, the stairs were special to him for some reason, and I spied a grin under his seaman's whiskers as he brought us around to see them. This is also when Tom's nerdy side reared its wild head. As the path came into view, Tom realized exactly what he was looking at. It was the path Rey took in *Star Wars: The Force Awakens*. We'd seen the spot from overhead in the monastery, guessing where Mr. Abram's had green-screened the Millennium Falcon, but this confirmed it all for Tom, and he lost his mind.

"Guys! It's Rey's path! It's Rey's path," he shouted, bouncing up and down.

As the path came into view,
Tom realized exactly what he was looking at. . . .
"Guys! It's Rey's path! It's Rey's path,"
he shouted, bouncing up and down.

He giggled, pointed, and clapped like a silly schoolgirl. He called back to our friend Luke to catch the sight on camera, but his rantings were jumbled. No one on the boat knew our names, so they must have wondered, *Is he calling out to Luke Skywalker?*

"Luke," he cried, "Luke, look! It's Rey's path!"

The folks around us laughed at his absurdity.

Pat Joe gave this scene time to play out and then took us on a similar tour of Lesser Skellig. After this, we had a forty-five-minute ride back to the mainland, whirring motor and dipping waves lifting us, once again, out of space and time. But unlike our trip out, now my heart and mind were primed for reflection. In fact, a reserve had built up and now my tinker spirit unlocked the door to engage the rest of me, and I found Jesus on a boat in the Atlantic Ocean.

BEN'S POINT OF VIEW

The idea of getting to conquer the island with my brothers was absolutely exciting. Robbie and I were on a different boat as we were last-minute additions and weren't guaranteed a ticket out to the island. As we were about ten minutes from departure to the island, we were told that there was no room for us and that we'd need to exit the boat so that the people who originally had tickets could take their spots.

At first I remember being disappointed that I couldn't join the guys, yet I was super excited for them to get out to the island and conquer it. As I walked up to their boat to say good-bye, I remember seeing their faces full of excitement, resolve, and wonder with a tad bit of fear hidden behind those same looks. I remember thinking that I could either complain to them or I could just try to be encouraging to them. I had a really quick mental flashback just thinking about all that it took for our team to get to this point in our journey and all the obstacles that had to be overcome in order to get to this point. This was not only a result of hard work put in but the definite provision and faithfulness of the Lord.

There was way too much to celebrate and be expectant for as the Lord had paved the way for us to be here. There was nothing that was going to stop them, and all that was needed was a bit of affirmation. . . . Plus, I'd heard there were castles nearby for Robbie and me to explore.

17

THE VIEW
FROM HERE

Jesus, the life-giving mason, sat himself across from me on the lip of our tiny boat, elbows on knees, smiling an ancient, subtle smile. He took a deep breath. So did I.

Your friends just carried you up a mountain, he said, and I laughed.

"Yeah, they did," I said silently. "They sure did. I'm floored by it."

What do you mean?

"I just can't wrap my head around exactly why they did it."

They love you.

We puttered past a puffin rolling on the waves like a buoy.

"Yeah, but why?" I'd just taken on a mountain. I might as well take on the hard questions next.

Why do they love you? he asked with a cocked eyebrow.

"Yeah," I said. "I mean, I'll never be able to do this for them. I'd like to, and I don't think they expect me to, but . . . I can't give back. And I've not done anything to prompt the love. I don't deserve any of this, for any reason. There's really just no grounds for it."

The question, and the truth behind it, settled deeper into my chest than ever before, and I let it continue to sink like a rock. I would not shy away. My life is perpetually painted with this question, but I was now thrust into a reckoning. Jesus sat quietly, watching that rock—that truth—sink. He could see it clearly and would be patient, as always, with it. He'd seen rocks before, been part of this process a hundred times over, truth settling into the hearts of men. He knew it well, from the throne to the cross and back again.

Why do I love you? he asked finally.

Tears pooled up in my eyes as I let out another laugh. "I have no idea!" I said.

I thought of his death. I thought of his walk on earth. I thought of his hands in the dirt, forming Adam. Nowhere in there was a reason, only the expression of his unbelievable love.

I love you, Kevan, he said, *because I want to. That's it.*

The rock landed softly in my belly and became a seed, "the implanted word, which is able to save souls." It was simple, but true and full as a tree. It brought life and satisfaction. I was loved because of a love unchanging, unwavering, and joyfully crazy about me. And the rest filled itself in, for as I knew Christ's love for me,

I found that love compelling me forward. My friends, too, were driven by the love of Christ for them, in them. They were driven unexplainably to carry me (literally) through the impossible. Not because I'm cool or because I'm an inspiration to them, but because of a true love beyond themselves, beyond any of us. And this had put us on a wonderful adventure across the known world.

My friends, too, were driven by the love of Christ for them . . .
to carry me (literally) through the impossible.
Not because I'm cool or because I'm an inspiration to them,
but because of a true love beyond themselves.

Tom shifted and the pain in my foot seemed to cry, "What about me?" Ah yes, such a good God! But then, why pain? "If you called us to climb, and you prepared the way, then why this one great, screaming caveat? Why not smooth sailing?" Sure, I was asking about the immediate, but the question pressed further in. I reflected on the day, on the trip as a whole, and saw the "sailing" for its true nature. It hadn't all been smooth. I cringed at memories of hitting my head on the subway, and laughed about our run across Paris, chasing a train we'd never catch. Finances had been provided; we'd gotten a lot of attention; the team had all stayed relatively healthy. But we still had mix-ups with money, we got lost and ran late more than we cared to admit, and everyone on the team felt the strain of our journey. And then there was this old foot and face of mine.

I looked at Tom, his shoulders before me, and I saw his act of love did not counter my pain, or diminish it. My pain was even made greater, I dare say, by his love. Injured, I could have stayed in bed and healed without consequence. I could have stayed home altogether and never gotten hurt. But look at the wide world I would've missed! Yes, his act of love carried me on. And the same act of love from Philip, Robbie, and Ben bore me into a light I'd have otherwise never know, and its warmth far succeeded any throb I'd acquired in the going.

There is a moment in C. S. Lewis's *The Lion, the Witch, and the Wardrobe* when Susan asks a beaver if the legendary lion Aslan is safe. Mr. Beaver chuckles at the question. "Who said anything about safe? 'Course he isn't safe. But he's good. He's the King, I tell you." Our good Father is full of life, full of adventure, and he's invited us into it—we were made for it, in fact!—but adventure, my friend, is never safe.

Your friends just carried you up an island, Jesus said again, giddy with the truth.

He gripped the boat's edge with his thick hands and sat up straight, stretching his back. He looked out over the waters, the Irish breeze playing in his hair.

"It hurt," I added, not complaining, just stating.

He nodded in full agreement.

"It hurt," I continued, "but none of this was normal, anyway, right?"

Jesus nodded again, more emphatically now, and broke into a grin from ear to ear.

I am a cripple, small and frail, feeble. I'm supposed to sit in a wheelchair. That's safe. I'm supposed to take supplements and maybe work on a computer. But instead, I let a bunch of medically unqualified musicians (God help 'em!) put me in a backpack and carry me around the world. Foolishness, really. Yeah, it was bound to hurt, but I'm alive. And I've seen the world as we all were meant to see it—big and beautiful and full of life.

I'm supposed to sit in a wheelchair.
That's safe. . . . But instead,
I let a bunch of medically unqualified musicians
(God help 'em!) put me in a backpack
and carry me around the world.

Chuck Colson once said, "A relationship with Jesus is an invitation into reality," an invitation to see the world, to experience life, as we were meant to before the fall. Jesus, after all, came that we "might have life, and have it more abundantly." Adventure like you've always wanted, life to the hilt, to the fullest full, happens when Jesus "carries" you. And that's going to hurt, because barricades drop and steps are high to reach, but that's adventure for you, and he will carry you through it. Who said anything about safe? But it will be good, because he is good. "He will never leave you, nor forsake you" in this Skellig-island life, and what's more, he will faithfully see you to the good, good end. He's the King, I tell you.

* * *

We came into the bay and the motor shut off less than a mile from port. People waited there for us, and we could see their confusion matched ours. What was this? Pat Joe came shuffling out from the helm and announced his intentions.

"Okay," he said quickly. "This's settle-up time, when ya pay meh."

Philip had our cash, so we were fine with it, but Tom couldn't help bursting into laughter. Tom had been talking about our skipper as though he couldn't hear him. Perhaps it was the language barrier, but he freely shared—with anyone—his observations of the man as they came to him.

"He's actually doing this," he cried. "He's holding us hostage till we pay! On a boat! In the ocean! This is fantastic!"

Pat Joe paid him no mind but shuffled around, collecting his due.

"I'm a middle school teacher," Tom explained to the baffled parent beside us. "You have no idea how many times I've wished I could do this to students, with homework or tests . . . never mind."

Once everyone paid, the motor sputtered to life and we closed the distance to land. Ben, Robbie, and Mr. Hill welcomed us at the pier, and we convened at the pub for lunch before hitting the road with drinks all around and fish and chips enough to feed an army. A handful of stories peppered the table, but it proved mostly a quiet time. What words could come so soon after the experience? Quiet was fine by us. We nodded to one another, grinned, offered cheers, and drank in the moment, every last drop.

TOM'S POINT OF VIEW

I've been on two major overseas trips now with Kevan and two smaller trips to California. That boat ride was the single most painful forty-five minutes we've spent together. I wanted Kevan to see as much as possible, and that meant he had to be on my back so I could turn and help him view whatever passed. But man alive! Sitting in a boat on those choppy waters with an extra eighty pounds on my back was almost too much. Next boat ride he will be in the pack strapped safely to the bow.

On a more serious note: I'm a terribly selfish person, and I know it has been with Kevan that I can remember the first moment of truly forgetting myself and thinking about someone else—if only for a few seconds at a time. It blows my mind that there are people born with that instinct of empathy and caregiving . . . people like nurses or firefighters or accountants.

18

REENTRY

Upon descending Skellig Michael, the pinnacle of our journey, my adrenaline ran out. Two and a half weeks (a year, if you include preparation) of energy and drive to reach this point, and when it was over, my body decided it'd had enough. I spent the remainder of our time in Ireland sleeping on a Dublin couch and ventured out only when the guys forced me to. The week came to a close and we caught a plane back to Paris, where we had one night before flying home to the States.

In the Dublin airport, we met a priest named Philip, who was on sabbatical. We sparked up a conversation with him, and he was encouraged by our endeavors, as we were by his. Arriving in Paris, we had another positive interaction, this time with a steward who brought us a wheelchair. I was in the backpack, so he didn't know—at first—what to do with himself. But we got to talking with him and he liked us, so he dubbed himself our personal guide through the airport. We gave him a "We Carry Kevan" sticker, and he immediately placed it on the wheelchair he'd brought. "Because he doesn't need it," he announced, pointing at me with a big smile, and I couldn't help but smile too. This was a man who truly understood.

I got to our hotel room at the airport and fell asleep for the afternoon. A few of the others had the same idea, but I found myself waking up in the company of those who did not. Ben and Philip were especially antsy, and Tom was ready as ever to give our beloved Paris one last hurrah. And here is a thing to be said of Tom: he has the uncanny ability to convince me to do anything. We speak the same language, you might say, and he knows my triggers. So, after a few back-and-forths—

"I'm so tired, dude."

"But, Kevan, it's Paris!"

—I found myself in the backpack and we were on our way back into the heart of the city. A great deal of the convincing, to let you in on a secret, came with the decision to revisit familiar places. I am a sucker for familiarity.

The four of us took the Tube into Paris and came out on the canal, around Notre Dame. First things first: find some of our old favorite food, Turkish kabobs in France. It felt like ages since we'd had it. We feasted like kings in a little open-air shop down an alley-way, sharing plates of fries and greasy chicken. Then we procured for ourselves some bread and wine and took it down to the riverside.

We were not alone in this evening affair. Hundreds of folks, young and old, from all walks of life, gathered at the river with their picnics and drinks. Best friends or perfect strangers, you couldn't distinguish for the ease and gaiety of the scene. And we blended in just fine. This was fascinating to me, that we were no longer the bumbling tourists we'd been a few weeks earlier. We were now comfortable. We knew the city. We knew the feel of it, and it fit us like a favorite hat.

---

*Hundreds of folks, young and old, from all walks of life,
gathered at the river. . . . And we blended in just fine.
This was fascinating to me, that we were no longer
the bumbling tourists we'd been a few weeks earlier.*

When our bread was done (a glorious doing), we continued down the canal. Houseboats docked along the Seine's edge, and we dreamed of a world where these were our homes. We lingered, studying the floating homes, until music came drifting and caught our ears.

Sounds of a jazz quartet trickled down from a nearby bridge, and we followed it upward like a prince after Rapunzel. But the band was just wrapping up as we came to it. We found before us, though, a man in his late thirties, playing guitar. He stood, scruffy, in the middle of the bridge and folks sat around him, listening to his songs. He played ballads from the '60s to the '90s and everything in between, especially featuring The Strokes and The Smiths, as his leather-jacket vocal style fit best in their range.

This was our setting for the rest of the evening. We sat ourselves down on the sidewalk with everyone else and took in our surroundings. The bridge was thru-traffic during the day, but as the sun set (at least today), it became exclusively a footbridge. The jazz band packed up while our guitarist sang his songs. And while he did his thing, another man came rolling by with a sleek, black upright piano. The pianist, without a word, set up farther down the bridge and waited his turn.

Finally, the guitarist ended his set, rattling off his name and thanks in both English and French, and it was time for the pianist. The guitarist had suited this world, grungy and roaming in his spirit, smoking and swaggering to boot, but the pianist was proper, educated, classical, and his presence raised standards wherever he went, I was sure of it. As the guitarist packed up his effects, the pianist laid his long fingers silently, elegantly, upon the keys before him. The moment of truth. What would come from the stoic royal and his clavier?

A crash of strings, crisp and rushing, broke like horses from the polished wooden box. The man's wrists flew. His fingers ran wild. The solo symphony poured out over the bridge, over those walking and those sitting, and all looked on in wonder. The stark image rang out a sound that changed the course of that whole spinning world.

We sat through a few waves of the performance and then

decided we should head back to the hotel. It was getting late and an early morning lay ahead.

* * *

Our train ride back carried us into a conversation that I'd held at bay for long enough: What comes next? What are we doing after this trip?

When we first decided to go on this adventure, to raise funds and step out into the unknown, we wondered if it would even happen. Then we got attention and everything went nuts! And I am a forward thinker. I lose touch with the present as my imagination dives headlong into what's next. That, I decided, would not do for this trip. I needed to be present for the journey and the buildup to it, or there'd be no point to any of it. So the question of what would come next had to be suppressed until later, and now we had reached *later*. The question could now be asked and was asked by all of us.

"We can't just keep doing stuff for you," Ben said pointedly. "People will get bored with it."

So the question of what would come next had to be suppressed until later, and now we had reached later. . . . "We can't just keep doing stuff for you," Ben said pointedly. "People will get bored with it."

"Well, yeah," I agreed. "And I don't want it to be all about me anyway."

There had been loose talk along the way of future trips and a nonprofit, but it was time to actually entertain those ideas.

"I feel like we've gone through this process," Tom said, "and now we can help others through it too."

"Right," I said. "That's what I'd like to do."

We had heard from so many folks already. People disabled, or friends of the disabled, reaching out to ask about our backpack and our plans. Others simply writing to express their encouragement in seeing us go for it. All new relationships that we wanted to foster and work with to some capacity. We could design backpacks, help plan trips, train folks to work together as a caregiving team. There were so many ways we might continue the legacy of this adventure.

It felt good to speak of such things and realize that the end of our journey might actually be just the beginning. We dug into more details on what a nonprofit would look like and where else we'd like to go. The world flew by outside. It had opened itself up to us, and we stepped in with no plans of ever turning back.

* * *

Soon we were back at the hotel, ordering pizza and calling it a night. And what a full, good night it had turned out to be.

The next morning we parted ways with Robbie, who had a different flight, and boarded our plane back to Atlanta. The nice thing about an early flight westward is that we ended up back in the States by the early afternoon of the same day.

We had taken with us a spare backpack, in case anything were to happen to "Harv" on the trip. And in the end, we decided to give it to the Parker family upon our return home. So, landing in Atlanta, we met up with them again—a perfect bookend to our journey—and gave Karson the gift. As it turned out, we never needed it, but it had gone everywhere with us.

The globetrotting backpack was bequeathed to our friend and his family, giving Karson the possibility of a new view of the world. His family has a new perspective too, seeing the world with their son fully in it, unhindered by his disabilities. Even now, we receive pictures and updates from them as they hike around Georgia and beyond. My favorite pictures are those of Karson on his dad's back, smiling ear to ear, with his hands clasped across Kris's equally joyful face.

We had taken with us a spare backpack,
in case anything were to happen to "Harv" on the trip.
And in the end, we decided to give it
to the Parker family upon our return home . . .
giving Karson the possibility of a new view of the world.

Karson is part of their adventures, right in the heart of it all, and he's loving every minute of it. So are his parents and his brothers.

And their adventure is life, lived together in freedom to go whenever and wherever they want, their whole family—everyone.

This, I thought to myself as we hugged them good-bye. *This is what it's all about.*

KRIS AND BRANDI'S POINT OF VIEW

We are incredibly grateful to Kevan and for the way his generosity is allowing Karson to take on new adventures in ways we never dreamed possible. Having the pack allows our family to enjoy hikes and nature without Karson having to be left behind. We've always loved being outdoors, but as Karson grew, it became increasingly difficult to continue to enjoy these activities.

Kevan pursuing his dreams has carried over into the way we dream for Karson. It reminded us again that Karson's needs aren't a barrier for the things we enjoy, but rather an obstacle for us to overcome together. That's a gift that can never be repaid.

Epilogue

THERE AND BACKPACK AGAIN

SEVEN HUNDRED AND EIGHTY-TWO DAYS after returning home from Europe, our team set out on another adventure, this time to China. As we realized in France especially, what we were doing didn't always need words to explain it. The image was enough, crossing linguistic chasms and penetrating cultural barriers without us having to say much, if anything. People saw one man carrying another, and they saw a group of friends living so intentionally and with so much joy. People saw this, and you could almost watch it click somewhere deep inside them. So we decided to push this envelope, to go somewhere so drastically different from our own Western, English-speaking world, and trust the image to still be enough.

In a place where disabilities were said to be shunned, hidden, and frowned upon, our aim was to be a spectacle. Let them stare— we were counting on it—and as they stared, let a seed be planted and a change of mind and heart come up from the soil. This was our prayer as we considered China with patience. After all, we had no door at the time to go through for this kind of vision, and that was something we knew only the Lord could provide.

Enter the wonderful work of Show Hope. In 2003, Mary Beth and Steven Curtis Chapman founded the organization to provide adoption aid grants that would enable a greater number of waiting children to enter loving families through adoption. As Show Hope's work broadened, they began to open Care Centers in China to help provide for the needs of orphans with acute medical and special needs through a partnership with New Hope Foundation. The first of these Care Centers—Maria's Big House of Hope—was named in honor of the Chapmans' youngest daughter who tragically passed in 2008. Maria's is a remarkable place.

I grew up listening to Steven Curtis Chapman, *The Great Adventure* being the first cassette I ever bought with my own money. Steven had promoted Show Hope over the years, so I was familiar with their family's story and ministry. As we considered our vision for China, I wondered if perhaps this could be our door.

Since returning from Europe, the team and I had gone head-long into developing a nonprofit ourselves. We called it We Carry Kevan, and our mission statement was (and still is), "Believing in the inherent value of every person, we mobilize individuals with disabilities by redefining accessibility as a cooperative effort." To what capacity this meant at the time, we weren't entirely sure, but for starters we knew it involved telling our story and getting our backpack into as many hands as possible. We wanted to provide opportunities for others to experience what we had, not just in travel but more so in the life-giving power of friendship.

Doors started opening to speak around the country, and Deuter was more than happy to help with the backpack side of things. Opportunities came to share at every kind of venue, from churches to pharmaceutical conferences, bouncing around North America, from east coast to west and back several times. At the same time, we worked with the Deuter company on building a professional version of the backpack we used on our trip. They would put together a prototype and send it to us, we'd try it out and then Skype with their German office to work out the kinks, and then they'd send another prototype, followed by another call, and so on and so forth.

It was a rich season we enjoyed, but amidst all of it, China was still just an idea lingering and nagging me like an itch until it came full tilt in February 2017 during one of my infamous visits to Nashville. Ben was with me this time, and we were spending the afternoon at a mall where our friend Roman insisted we go for the best donuts in town. Exploring the area, I noticed Show Hope's office was there! Great! I was tempted to go up on a cold call, but where would I begin? To access their office, you had to press a buzzer and declare your intent for being there. "Hi, I'm a guy in a wheelchair, and last year my friends carried me around Europe in a backpack, and now . . ." I had a funny feeling that wouldn't fly as a first impression.

"Lord, they're right there," I prayed as I joined Roman and Ben in the coffee shop downstairs. "If this is the door, you're going to have to open it. I need you to make the introductions."

Just then, a guy with black-rimmed glasses and well-coiffed hair passed by the coffee shop entrance. He suddenly paused, backed up, and glanced in at my friends and me. He pulled his phone from his pocket, scrolled through its contents, then walked in to greet us. His brow twisted in a mix of confusion and humor as he approached.

"So," he said slowly, "you were on my phone this morning."

The day before, we had gone for a hike with a friend, and he'd posted a photo of it online, which this guy had seen. We had a laugh about it as we made introductions. His name was Phil Shay, and as it turned out, he was the director of donor engagement for Show Hope, which meant he was involved in setting up trips for folks interested in visiting the Care Centers in China. Isn't it funny, God's timing? I went right into explaining to Phil what we wanted to do with Show Hope, and he was thrilled to take us upstairs to meet the rest of the office. It turned into a sort of water cooler pitch— "Tell them what you told me. . . . Okay, now tell them, too . . . and them." Within just a few minutes, we had lifelong friendships blooming with the staff, including Cathy Troyer and Mindy Cook, who became integral to our planning over the next several months.

Now that there was a door, we had to figure out who would go through it with me. Tom, Ben, and Luke were given returners. I wouldn't have done the first trip without them, and I wouldn't do this one without them either. There was a matter of finding more carriers, as well as filling some other roles we foresaw. We needed a manager, for example. While we had pulled off the first trip, this level of organization and financing was not too strong a suit for any of us. My Uncle "Captain" Fritz Christo was, however, the man for such a job, working as a Project Manager for the Canadian government. He gladly came on board to handle logistics from home base, and he brought with him a sixteen-year-old Chinese-Canadian as the much-needed translator for our journey. Philip and Robbie had moved on in their careers, but Mr. Hill was interested in joining us again for Round 2. We also invited our friend Dan Tenney to join as our third carrier. His background in military medicine meant he really counted as our third and fourth carriers, like if Captain America and Bruce Willis had a baby, so we felt confident about our assembled team.

Unfortunately, about a month before our departure, the top floor of Mr. Hill's house burned down in an electrical fire. Then, the week before we left, Dan had a family emergency come up that required his attention. Suddenly, our ranks were shrinking. I was admittedly getting a bit worried. Thankfully, our globetrotting friend Marcus Miller (a bald man with the lanky features of a rock climber) was up for the last-minute venture. Our team of six met up in Vancouver on August 30, 2018, and flew out to encounter the wide, old world of China.

We had settled on dividing our time between three cities, beginning with our translator's family home in Guilin and going from there to visit Maria's in Luoyang, and then New Hope Foundation in Beijing. And in each of these cities, we also had one hike planned.

First, we climbed Elephant Trunk Hill in Guilin, then explored the Shaolin Temple near Luoyang, and finally walked a section of the Great Wall in Beijing. While these physical exploits were full of fun and profound danger, the real treasures—the true adventures— of this trip were found in our interactions with people.

* * *

Our flight from Vancouver carried us across the Pacific and down to Shanghai, then over a short jump to Guilin. Grandpas 3 and 6 picked us up from the airport and Grandpa 1 greeted us at the house. According to our translator, Grandpa 1 was the eldest of eight brothers and was his actual grandfather. Grandpas 3, 6, and 8 and their wives joined us throughout the week as well, and they were what we would call great uncles, numbered for their place in the age line.

The house we stayed in was sort of a vacation home, available for anyone in their family to use. A concrete structure boasting thirteen bedrooms, it has two levels with open air space down the middle and a set of great wooden doors hanging at the entrance. The size of these doors suggests security and guardianship, like a fortress, but they swung lazily open and the neighbor folks meandered through them at all hours.

We found ourselves in a rural area (potentially the first white people to ever set foot there), deep in a range of mountains like stalagmites shrouded in trees and brush. Our translator explained the legend of these mountains, that an emperor long ago wanted to fill the ocean with rock. He enslaved the local people to do this.

As they worked, an elderly woman came looking for her son, and the workers helped in her search. She wove her hair together into a cord as a gift to the people for their kindness, and like a whip it could drive the stone to do their will. Hungry for power, the emperor took the cord for himself and used it recklessly, whipping the earth without regard, and the result was this range of peculiar pillars of earth, shrub, and stone. Rivers and roads wove between the mountains, and a ways off one of these roads, tucked between a pond and mountain, set our open fortress home, where we rested from our flights and prepared for the adventures ahead.

While these physical exploits were full of fun and profound danger, the real treasures— the true adventures—of this trip were found in our interactions with people.

Travels to our next two cities brought us to the playroom floors of Maria's in Luoyang and New Hope Foundation's Beijing Care Center. We were happy to see our team grow as well. It went from six to more than thirty, including carriers, translators, and simply new, likeminded friends.

At Maria's, we found kindred spirits in those serving there. Katie, Michaela, Rose, and Sarah were all our family that week as we delved into a full life with them in the Care Center. We rolled around on mats with the kiddos, explored the city, and talked over meals about books, movies, and living in service to others.

There were visitors, too, from the stateside Show Hope office. The morning after arriving, we came downstairs to find none other than Phil Shay coming through the front door with a team of donors and Show Hope's liaison at Maria's, Nate. Both men were broad-shouldered and, as the week unfolded, pitched in to carry me. We ventured together into the market streets, where they took the helm to navigate our wandering posse through hordes of pedestrians and herds of food trucks (literally, hundreds of them).

This same night of braving the market, Ben was carrying me after dinner and one of our friends (most likely Katie, who knew the city well), suggested we go into the park across the street. It was a well-lit, paved area where folks gathered for Kung Fu demonstrations and music was often playing. Just a fun scene to experience in the downtown Luoyang nightlife. Little did we know Ben and I were about to turn it on its head.

Our crew—twelve of us—meandered over and spread out as we came under the lights. A boom box sat in the center of the park, a dance beat protruding from its thirty-year-old speakers. Ben couldn't resist. His footsteps moved into the rhythm, his hips (my feet attached) started to sway, his elbows bent and fingers began to snap. A few people glanced at us in curiosity. It wasn't long before a man with graying hair and swimming eyes ran up and implored us with gestures to follow him. He took us about fifty yards to the side, where he had his own DJ set up with speakers and hyperactive dance beats ready to go. As we came closer, the DJ cranked up his tunes and the man broke into psychedelic dancing from head to toe. I couldn't stop laughing, and Ben couldn't either, but he saw an opportunity and took it. Whatever move the man made, Ben mirrored it as best he could, treating it like a sort of dance-off—or he was just trying to keep up in the crazy whirlwind moment. As for me, I was back in Paris again, and I adopted the same philosophy as I had then—go limp and just enjoy the ride.

A boom box sat in the center of the park,
a dance beat protruding from its thirty-year-old speakers.
Ben couldn't resist. His footsteps moved into the rhythm,
his hips (my feet attached) started to sway.

It was liberating to spin and shake, to lean this way and swoop that way, to lose ourselves in the blaring beats. I kept my eyes open, though, and between the blur of our movements, I noticed people were gathering around. And they weren't joining in; they were watching, their cell phones out, filming us, the spectacle. Within seconds, a crowd of twenty had encircled us. Then forty, fifty, a hundred. They just kept coming, and soon I couldn't see the back of the crowd. Ben focused solely on the man he was mirroring, so what was a blur to me hardly even existed to him. He kept dancing, the crowd kept coming, and I kept laughing at the pure absurdity of it all.

Twice, Ben slowed down to check on me, asking if I was all right. I answered that I was fine, and the first time he went back to dancing, but the second time he settled in to what was happening around us. Then he finally saw how the crowd had grown to mob status and people were getting a little more interactive. He shook the hand of our dancing friend and began to push through the mass of people. As we did, they grabbed at our limbs and clothes and pressed closer. We waded through to Tom and Marcus, who took up the role of bodyguards as we headed across the park to leave, with the rest of our crew following along with the entire crowd. Ben looked back only for a second to see the flock coming, and with a cry of surprise he doubled our speed. We made it to the street before being surrounded again, then with our people helping, we pushed through, crossed traffic, and jumped into our car.

In Beijing, the good people at New Hope Foundation took us in as their own. Rob and Joyce founded the center some thirty years ago, Joyce being a doctor and seeing ways to serve children in need. They live on campus, working full time with unconditional love for the thousands of children who come through their doors. Joyce kindly gave us a tour of their facility and shared stories of God's faithfulness over the years, how he had showed up in amazing ways to provide for the needs of "the babies" (as she calls all of the children), bringing healing and hope to so many. Rob had lunch with us, relaying a great deal of these same stories himself and with as much joy. The team they've built up and work alongside are people of gentle spirits, young families with life in their eyes and generosity in their smiles.

While in Beijing, we also took a hike along the Great Wall, which ended up being—we calculated later—the equivalent of 102 stories worth of stairs, almost double the steps of Skellig Michael and far surpassing it in time and difficulty. Much of this intensity may be attributed to Tom, our terrific instigator, who knows how to push me beyond safety into what he cryptically refers to as "what we came for." In this case, we reached a barrier on the wall with a sign declaring the end of the restored path. Beyond the barrier rose another several hundred steps high into the clouds. Tom found a low section to hop over, and since I was on his back, I found myself on the back side of a "CAUTION" sign and scaling more steps into the unknown. I have hiked with Tom long enough to still argue . . . but maybe not as deliberately as I used to.

While in Beijing, we also took a hike along the Great Wall, which ended up being—we calculated later— the equivalent of 102 stories worth of stairs, almost double the steps of Skellig Michael.

Every two or three hundred yards, a shelter stood, a watchtower in its heyday, and so we paused at one for a rest. I sat on the stone floor and took in the breathtaking view. The guys scattered for the moment to take in views themselves. It was in this time that Tom wandered further up the path of the Great Wall before returning, panting and drenched in even more sweat than before (impossible as that might have seemed to all involved).

"Kevan," he said between gasps of air. "If you'll just humor me for another two hundred yards—"

"I dunno," I said, looking out over the endless green mountains. "What did you find?"

"What we came for," he said with a smirk.

"We've already come a long way, man," I said. "I'm pretty content."

We had covered a few miles so far. We couldn't even see the place we'd started from anymore. I figured, if I hadn't had enough, the guys probably had. So, I was genuinely satisfied and ready to head back, no matter what Tom had found. That's what I told myself anyway.

"Well, I brought a video to give you an idea," he replied, pulling out his phone.

"No," I protested. "I don't want to see it."

My logic was that if we were going, I didn't want the video to spoil it, and if we weren't going, I didn't want to know what I missed. I was secretly having a hard-enough time saying no, though my body was done for the day and my responsible side tried to hold its ground. As we debated, Ben returned and Tom showed him the video.

"Oh yeah," Ben agreed with raised eyebrows. "Don't show him that!"

"Wait," I started. "Why not?"

Did he not want the video to spoil it or did he not want me to know what I would miss? Did he think I'd want to go against his will, or did he want to go and assumed the video would deter me? So much mystery, I couldn't handle it! Tom and Ben broke into laughter as I got worked up and gave a final, resolute answer.

"Alright," I announced. "Let's go!"

We emerged from the watchtower and continued along the wall, a wide, smooth path.

I wasn't impressed.

"Is this it?" I asked. "Tom, this isn't really a big deal."

"Not a big deal?" he roared over his shoulder to me. "Not a big deal? Kevan! We're in China! On the Great Wall!"

"Right right right," I clarified amidst the barrage of everyone's shared sentiment. "I just mean this is like the rest of the hike, what we've covered already."

"We're getting there," he said, pointing ahead.

Sure enough, after a few more yards, the Wall's degradation became more apparent. Bricks were loose, pieces cracked or gone completely, and a little further along, the majority of it was fallen away entirely. Now there was no turning back. Tom was right— in regard to our hike, this was exactly what we had come for. Trees grew up high around us, offering their limbs for balance as we made our way along a row of ten-inch-wide stone with bottomless drop-offs on either side. In one or two spots, we created a support system, with Ben holding branches, Marcus holding Ben, and Tom (carrying me) using them both for stability as we stepped high over boulders or up onto a dubious brick.

Finally, we reached a clearing where the wall came back together, and we took in the view around us. The wild, green mountains of China rose and fell through clouds below. Once again, our ragamuffin posse had scaled the impossible together to see the world anew.

Yet, for all of our high-flying thrills and wonderful moments of camaraderie, the most shining hours of our time in China were spent with the children being cared for at the Care Centers. We took with us, in a giant green duffle bag, two additional backpacks to donate if they proved beneficial. And if we had known just how well they would be received, we'd have taken a hundred more! At both Maria's and the Beijing Care Center, little ones who would otherwise never be able to walk rose up high on the shoulders of their nannies to see the world from a whole new view.

Sometime after our dance in the park, and long before our hike along the Great Wall, we sat in an empty playroom. Actually, I laid on a mat on the floor. Ben, Marcus, Tom, and Luke paced. My backpack sat in the middle of the room. We waited. Just an hour earlier, we had shown one of the extra backpacks to some of the folks at Maria's—Michaela, Katie, and a few others. Our plan was to break down the various aspects of it for them to understand inside-out, then introduce it to a few of the kids the next day. But as soon as Michaela—the resident physical therapist—tried it on for herself, her face lit up.

"I wanna try it today," she said, nearly trembling with excitement. "And I know exactly who to try it with!"

She said the little girl's name and everyone agreed. It was Michaela's idea to start with one child away from the others. This would be a lot to take in anyway, a new thing, so it was best to make her comfortable and ease her into it. We limited who would be in the room to just me, the guys, her nanny, and a few others she was closest to. So we boys waited in an empty playroom for the girls to bring in the little one.

Suddenly, a stream of sweet voices came trickling down the hallway. Katie opened the door and Michaela came in after her, holding the little girl, a spunky sprite with eyes full of mischief. Rose and one of the nurses came in quietly, too, and stood back by the door along with our translator, giving Michaela and Katie space with her to settle into the room. We followed their lead and backed away. Michaela sat on a mat with the fairy girl in her lap, jabbering on and tickling her till giggles filled the room while Katie collected some favorite toys for her to play with.

Yet, for all of our high-flying thrills and
wonderful moments of camaraderie,
the most shining hours of our time in China
were spent with the children
being cared for at the Care Centers.

After a few minutes, they decided she was acclimated and ready for some introduction to the new thing. Michaela, still holding her, pointed toward me and in Mandarin said, "Who's that? That's my friend Kevan!" The girl had seen me the day before, so she was fine. Michaela went on to explain to her that I couldn't walk, like her. "So, how does he get around?" They both looked around for an answer until Michaela pointed to the backpack. This was the cue for Ben and Marcus to put me in my backpack, strap me in, and get me up on Ben's back, all in view of those spritely eyes. As Michaela and Katie explained what we were doing, the girl's eyes watched carefully. Once I was up, I waved down at her and trotted around goofily with Ben while Katie cheered us on.

"Do you want to try?" came next as they showed her the other pack, open and ready for her, but she refused.

At the sight of the other pack, at the revelation that it was her turn to try, the little fairy tucked herself deep into Michaela's arms and shook her head. Michaela held her close, and Katie stroked her cheek, asking softly what was the matter. She wouldn't have it, though, wouldn't give an answer, wouldn't even look at the thing. Tears welled up from deep inside her tender heart, and Michaela carried her off to the corner to calm down. Rose stepped in to help and took her for a moment of comfort, rocking her gently.

With the nurse came tottering in another little girl, her shadow. She was able to walk on her own and, bravely, went right up to the open pack, even trying to climb into it by herself. We all laughed and shrugged—Why not?! Michaela, Katie, and the nurse got her in and secured, Tom nearby to help if needed. They lifted her onto Michaela's back and the little adventurer's face beamed so that she was like the sun rising, so bright and beautiful. She chuckled as Katie and the nurse ran around the room with her, the fairy watching sulkily from Rose's arms. Ben and I joined in the party, and the one girl looked over to the other with a smile, as if to say, "It's okay! You'll love it!"

After several circles around the room, we brought her down and out of the pack, hoping her peer would be ready to try now. The nurse left with her while Michaela took the first back into her arms, but she was still nervous. Her nanny stepped in to ease her more. Marcus and Tom had moved toward the door, as had Rose. Ben and I followed, along with Luke and our translator, leaving the fairy girl alone with Michaela, Katie, and her nanny. In the hallway we paced, we sat, we waited. Conversations came and we were almost into other worlds when Marcus spoke up.

At the sight of the other pack, at the revelation
that it was her turn to try, the little fairy tucked herself
deep into Michaela's arms and shook her head.

"Hey, guys, she's in," and we all took a minute to believe him.

He peered in through the door window, but before any of us could get up to see, we heard it. Squeals of joy, songs of laughter, like those she had brought into the room before, but now even louder. Luke darted into the connected room, holding his camera over a bookshelf to spy, and the rest of us crowded around the door window. High up on her nanny's back, the little fairy giggled and shrieked with wonder as Katie and Michaela danced around her, life abundant and bursting from every corner of their games.

I stood at that window and watched as a child played hide-and-seek. I watched as she chased and tagged those who love her unconditionally, on the back of her nanny—a woman who says to her every day through action, "You are dear, you are lovely, you are wanted." A child whose beginnings carried so much disruption and loss, until her heavenly Father brought her into the loving arms of these caregivers. Redemption at its finest. And I couldn't believe we got to be part of this miracle. I was speechless—I still am—to think that a couple of buddies wanted to explore Europe and three years later, we were here, doing this; that Jesus pushed back against the Fall, and as his children we got to be participants in his redeeming, life-giving work; that we made a backpack for me to thrill-seek some sites, and now it was being used to further show a little girl just how very much she is dear, lovely, and wanted.

As the rest of our trip unfolded, we got to see this, got to be part of these kinds of moments, over and over again. We witnessed it again at Maria's and then at New Hope as well. And would you believe, it never got old, not for a second.

One afternoon in Luoyang, Katie took our team on an excursion to see the Shaolin Temple, where it is said Kung Fu was born. Tucked far up into the mountains, the temple was hidden from the world for hundreds of years and lost to a fire long ago. It was rediscovered in the twentieth century, restored where it could be, reconstructed where needed, and is now open to the public for visiting, worship, and study.

We toured the grounds, climbing steps to houses where this emperor visited one night when it rained or that monk lived after years of solitude in a cave. History lingered like a heavy blanket as we admired the structures and artwork, the brilliance of design and piety. The layout led us farther and farther back into this walled fortress, farther and farther up flights of stairs, passing monks and tourists alike who mingled without regard for one another. Finally, we reached the pinnacle, the very back of the ancient temple world, where a stone shelter stood wide, with great paneless windows overlooking the mountains. Our tour guide (a friend of Katie's) drew us closer to look inside.

"People come from all over the world," she said, "to see the temple. And while the rest of it is amazing and beautiful, everyone comes to stand where you're standing right now. They come to see this. Can you guess why?"

I couldn't believe we got to be part of this miracle.
I was speechless—I still am—to think that
a couple of buddies wanted to explore Europe
and three years later, we were here, doing this.

Artwork hung around the otherwise bare room. We asked about them and she explained their significance.

"But that's not why," she said, pushing up her glasses.

She then pointed dramatically to the floor. It was made up of thick stone slabs, and these slabs were dented in perfect rows, cracked and caved in, round pits several inches deep, a man's breadth in diameter. Our guide explained these were the result of monks practicing Kung Fu repeatedly on these spots for centuries, slamming their feet into the stone over and over. Four hundred years of stomping will leave an impression.

And this stayed with me through the rest of our journey, the image of those holes in the ground made by intentionality. You can stomp your foot once as hard as you want, and you'll have nothing to show for it. Maybe a bruised foot. But you stomp as hard as you can over and over for a lifetime, and then your children pick up where you left off, and their children too. There might be a dent left in a solid rock floor. It only happened in this temple because the practice mattered to those monks more than anything else. They repeated the motions day in and day out, driven by the disciplines of their faith, and we have these dents left after so long to show us how serious they were, how much the art of Kung Fu really mattered to them.

What matters to you? We are all stomping, day in and day out, investing our time and energy into what we've deemed most important. It is those things that will remain, those things that our children will carry on after us, those things that will form a you-sized crater in the stone floor over time. And the world will come to see, and they will say, "This was formed by repeated stomping."

What is your stomp? Is your bank account priority, or how you can best serve your neighbor? Are you more concerned with your son's GPA, or his relationship with the Lord? We are all stomping; we can't help it. As long as we're alive, we're leaving an impression. Sometimes it is intentional. Far too often it is not, but it doesn't have to stay that way.

My friends and I went on a trip, and they carried me in a backpack because we loved each other and we wanted to have the experience together, living life to the fullest, unhindered by our shortcomings. Now we find ourselves giving this opportunity to others—families, friends, orphans waiting to be adopted. Whether it's Denver, London, or Beijing, the Lord is taking us and making it clear what really matters. Across the board, folks are looking to love and be loved; longing to invite and be invited; searching for hope and hoping for something more.

As long as we're alive, we're leaving an impression.
Sometimes it is intentional. Far too often it is not,
but it doesn't have to stay that way.

We need Jesus, and we need each other, as God intended it to be from the beginning. When man fell into sin, not only did we separate from our Creator, but we separated from each other as well. This is why, in John's letters to the young church, he says that "the Word became flesh and dwelt among us" and "that which we have seen and heard we proclaim also to you, so that you too may have fellowship with us; and indeed our fellowship is with the Father and with his Son Jesus Christ." Communion with one another points us to the gospel, loving one another "as Christ loved us and gave himself up for us." And communion with Jesus aligns our hearts to love one another better until they "know us by our love."

The apostle Paul addresses stomping in one of his letters to Timothy. He says our aim is love. So this is our charge, our calling, not merely as Christians but as members of the human race, "all creatures of our God and King." This is our stomping, to love "in word and deed," pointing one another toward Jesus Christ, the Author of Salvation, Giver of Life, the Light of Man. This is where freedom, adventure, and community are found. This is how life is lived to the fullest, as it was intended from the beginning, with God and man together. This truly is what it's all about.

About Us

 **WE CARRY KEVAN**

ONE OF THE MANY THINGS that my friendship with Kevan has taught me is the power of a *request*—the power of asking for help. Our culture teaches us to value independence and self-sufficiency. We often hesitate from making requests of others because we don't want to be rude and encroach on other people's time and energy. Or, perhaps more often, we hesitate to ask for help because we don't want to be perceived by others as weak and vulnerable.

These hesitations are strange for those of us who call ourselves Christians. Jesus teaches us the simple and profound spiritual principle: "*Ask*, and you shall receive." Jesus taught us in the Lord's Prayer to make persistent requests. Our faith teaches us that we all have unique limitations and unique gifts. If we are going to flourish, we are told that we need to learn to ask for help from God and from others.

A request, rightly made, can be a powerful invitation into relationship. A request—the willingness to accept our limitations and to ask for help—enables us to accomplish things together that we cannot accomplish on our own. Far from being rude, asking for help should be seen as an invitation for others to bring their gifts and resources to bear in our own lives.

A couple weeks after Kevan returned from his trip to Europe, he sent me a text.

"Have any time to chat today? I'll be at Fortezza."

I was eager to hear about his trip, so I decided my sermon prep could wait until the next day. Besides, I rarely need my arm twisted to take a visit to my favorite coffee shop.

"Sure, I'll be down in an hour."

We sat outside together and I listened as Kevan told me some of his favorite stories about his remarkable journey, many that you've just finished reading about. And then Kevan told me what he had in mind next.

"I've been thinking about starting a non-profit that would help others do what my friends helped me to do. We've got a good thing with this backpack we've designed, and I'm thinking that we could get it into the hands of others who could use it. I've got some other ideas too. . . ."

I don't remember the specific ideas that he shared with me that day, but I do remember clearly thinking in my head, *I hope Kevan asks me to help him with this. I would love to be a part of this. Please ask me to help. Please ask me to help!* And he did!

In 2016 we, with our outstanding team, started a non-profit

called We Carry Kevan. Since then we have been working, planning, asking, praying, and strategizing to accomplish our mission:

BELIEVING IN THE INHERENT VALUE OF ALL PEOPLE,
WE CARRY KEVAN MOBILIZES INDIVIDUALS
WITH DISABILITIES BY REDEFINING
ACCESSIBILITY AS A COOPERATIVE EFFORT.

We are seeking to do this in at least three ways. First, we have worked with Deuter Sport to develop an innovative backpack designed specifically for carrying individuals with disabilities. In the Spring of 2019, the backpacks will be available worldwide. In addition to making them available for purchase, we want to provide backpacks to ministries like Show Hope all around the world.

Second, we are developing weekend events for individuals with disabilities and their care teams to cultivate imagination for new possibilities and to expand their capacity by bringing a wider community of people around them.

Third, we want to assist individuals with disabilities to experience the world as accessible through networks of friendship and cooperation. By planning trips and assisting others in planning their own adventures, we hope to connect able-bodied and disabled people across the globe.

After reading Kevan's story, I imagine you may be thinking, as I did on that day outside of Fortezza Coffee, *Please ask me to help!* So, I am going to put the lesson I've learned from Kevan into practice and make a request: Will you help us?

Please pray (right now!) for the work and mission of We Carry Kevan. We believe that our vision for accessibility through cooperation has the power to bring hope to millions of people. Please be a part of that by praying for us.

You can also help by being mindful of individuals with disabilities who go to your church or who live in your neighborhood. Allow Kevan's story to move you toward them. Friendship is one of the greatest gifts that you can offer. And if they haven't heard about Kevan's story, pass on a copy of the book to them.

Finally, let us know if you would like to volunteer to carry others, invite Kevan and his team to speak, financially sponsor backpacks and weekend events, or simply donate to our work. We are better together!

—Ryan Cochran
President of the Board, We Carry Kevan

For more information:

WeCarryKevan.com

Acknowledgments

THIS MEMOIR IS, in its own way, an entire book of acknowledgments. Every inch of my life—and this journey in particular—is only only only made possible by the countless friends and family around me, and even a few strangers along the way. The love and support I have received makes no sense to me, but I'm thankful nonetheless.

Mom and Dad decided to have me, for starters, and then raised me to live an abundant life; my brother, Andrew, made cardboard horses, capes, and toy airplanes to carry away my imagination; my sister, Connie, introduced me to Aslan before I could read his name myself. Tumnus, Pooh, and Danny Orlis were my cords of kindness; Inigo, Pan, and Auberon Quin have been my bands of love. As to living authors, Walter Moers told me to write; Walter Wangerin told me what was worth writing; Frederick Buechner told me how; and the Peterson boys made it all come alive with conversation and books of their own.

I have homes around the world, communities that I am tethered to and can only be away from for so long. I was born in South Florida, where the Perry family's house still has the same kitchen table and an open-door policy. I grew up around North Carolina, where southern churches and the local music scene defined my formative years; I find rest still amid those hills in the company of Iveys, Troyers, Cookes, Stapps, Almatrouds, and many other wonderful folks. Nowadays, I take my mail at a Fort Wayne, Indiana, coffee shop called Fortezza, where I spend most of my time with dear friends of all sorts; if I'm not there (and I'm in town), I can be found at either JK O'Donnell's pub or at "the Coop," the house of Ben Duvall, where I sleep and watch reruns of *The Office*. England has the Pococks, who welcome me and my gang into their home time and time again, and Lauren Morse, who carries in her book bag bananas and sunshine wherever she goes. Then there's Franklin, Tennessee, where I find myself every few months (sometimes weeks) for rest, inspiration, and joy among Bristows, Vedderses, Dorises, Troyers, Shays, the various Petersons, and the ever-faithful Roman Haviland. And finally, all across the globe from Canada to Australia, Mexico, and around the States, we have my beloved extended family, who carry on our Christian heritage with open arms and serving hands.

Day in and day out, guys from all walks of life help me with my personal needs. Bathing, dressing, eating, driving, using the restroom, reaching books, opening this pen, or lifting that glass. Currently, these ranks include: Ben Duvall, Matt Spurgeon, Ian Delaney, Drew Heiniger, Noah Huffman, Danny Tenney, Marcus

Miller, Nathan Miller, Jered Blanchard, Sean Wang, Reuben Schneider, Drew Taft, Toby Taylor, AJ Yoder, Jeremy Stroup, Ryan Cochran, Tony Fingerle, Steve Erick, Justus King, Jeff Bower, David Hammitt, Nickolas Harrington, Ayron King, Joe Maurer, Isaiah Barker, Josh Baxter, Roman Haviland, Joe Sutphin, Landon Ivey, Hayden Cooke, Luke Thompson, Tom Troyer, and Zach Lycans.

The masterminds behind this book are as follows: Pete Peterson offered and accomplished initial edits; Hayden Cooke, the Cochrans, the Hammitts, the Fingerles, Paul Danger, and Katrina Kirtz read early manuscripts; my dear sister, Connie, listened as I read aloud for editing purposes; Rachel Hammitt did cover design and interior formatting for early copies. Cathy Troyer passed it on to Wes Yoder, who has since become my friend and agent, guiding me through the publishing forest and other industry realms. The amazing folks at Worthy and Hachette have taken tremendous care of this book, bringing it not just to life but skipping like a calf loosed from its stall; working with editor Kyle Olund, in particular, has been great, as our trust and friendship has been forged over donuts at The Factory.

Ambassador Speakers, Show Hope, Deuter, Give Kids The World, Sunrise Medical, Fortezza, Bravas, Cinema Center, Joni & Friends, and Rabbit Room have all been so supportive, along with our local churches over these past few years as the book and ministry have come together. The same can be said for the board members and support team of our nonprofit, We Carry Kevan, which currently includes: Ryan Cochran, Tony and Maria Fingerle, Rick and Lori Gerig, Joe Schenke, Evan Nuebacher, Brittany Corner,

Ben Duvall, Luke Thompson, Katy Fulp, Rachel Hammitt, Wes Yoder, Paul Malhotra, Jen Flickenger, Erin Heck, Taylor Beaty, and Steve Linsenmayer.

It seems appropriate, too, to acknowledge Abba Father, who has created and redeemed every one of the aforementioned places and people, including me, for which I can never be grateful enough.

About the Author

KEVAN CHANDLER grew up in the foothills of North Carolina with his parents and two siblings. The youngest of the bunch, he was the second to be diagnosed with spinal muscular atrophy, a rare neuromuscular disease. He has a bachelor's of arts degree in counseling from John Wesley College. In the summer of 2016, Kevan and his friends took a trip across Europe, leaving his wheelchair at home, and his friends carried him for three weeks in a backpack. An avid storyteller, Kevan has authored several books and speaks worldwide about his unique life with a disability. He is also the founder of We Carry Kevan, a nonprofit striving to redefine accessibility as a cooperative effort.

For more information:
WeCarryKevan.com

For speaking requests:
AmbassadorSpeakers.com/site/schedule-a-speaker

IF YOU ENJOYED THIS BOOK, WILL YOU CONSIDER SHARING THE MESSAGE WITH OTHERS?

Mention the book in a blog post or through Facebook, Twitter, Pinterest, or upload a picture through Instagram.

Recommend this book to those in your small group, book club, workplace, and classes.

Head over to Facebook.com/WeCarryKevan, "LIKE" the page, and post a comment as to what you enjoyed the most.

Tweet "I recommend reading #WeCarryKevan by @WeCarryKevan // @worthypub"

Pick up a copy for someone you know who would be challenged and encouraged by this message.

Write a book review online.

WORTHY® PUBLISHING

Visit us at worthypublishing.com

twitter.com/worthypub

worthypub.tumblr.com

facebook.com/worthypublishing

pinterest.com/worthypub

instagram.com/worthypub

youtube.com/worthypublishing